THE ABSOLUTELY TRUE DIARY OF A PART-TIME INDIAN

Sherman Alexie

AUTHORED by Jessica LeAnne Jones
UPDATED AND REVISED by A. Boghani

COVER DESIGN by Table XI Partners LLC
COVER PHOTO by Olivia Verma and © 2005 GradeSaver, LLC

BOOK DESIGN by Table XI Partners LLC

Published by GradeSaver LLC, www.gradesaver.com

First published in the United States of America by GradeSaver LLC. 2015

ISBN 978-1-60259-509-5

Printed in the United States of America

For other products and additional information please visit
http://www.gradesaver.com

Table of Contents

Biography of Sherman Alexie (1966–N.A.)

Sherman Alexie is an award-winning author, poet, and filmmaker. His work primarily focuses on contemporary Native American identity.

Alexie was born on October 7, 1966 on the Spokane Indian Reservation in Washington, to Sherman Joseph Alexie and Lillian Agnes Cox. He is of Coeur d'Alene, Colville, Flathead, Spokane, and Caucasian descent. Alexie has spoken about how deeply his father's alcoholism affected him, and his work often explores the effects of alcoholism on the reservation. After seeing the way addiction robbed many of his friends and family members of their aspirations, Alexie made the choice to avoid alcohol.

In his early life, Alexie suffered from poor health. He was born with Hydrocephalus (colloquially referred to as "water on the brain"), a serious medical condition in which fluid accumulates in the brain cavities and can result in abnormal enlargement of the head, possible mental disability, or even death. Alexie underwent a successful surgery when he was six months old that saved him from the more serious symptoms of his condition, but his classmates frequently mocked him for his enlarged head. Furthermore, he suffered from seizures and had to refrain from participating in physical activities on the reservation, which alienated him from other boys his age.

Despite his physical difficulties, Sherman Alexie excelled academically and eventually enrolled in a public high school outside the reservation. His success in the classroom and on the basketball court earned him a scholarship to Gonzaga University in 1985, where he planned to study medicine and law. Two years later, Alexie discovered that he was unhappy with his chosen fields and transferred to Washington State University. Unsure of his career path, Alexie attended literature classes at his new university and found his life's calling under the tutelage of Professor Alex Kuo, a noted poet and author who served as Alexie's literary mentor.

Kuo inspired Sherman Alexie to begin writing. His first published work, *The Business of Fancydancing: Stories and Poems,* came out in 1992. In 2002, it was adapted into a film that Alexie wrote and directed; it received mixed reviews. Alexie's first prose novel, *The Lone Ranger and Tonto Fistfight in Heaven*, was published in 1993 and received the PEN/Hemingway Award for Best First Book of Fiction. *Reservation Blues*, the sequel to *Lone Ranger,* came out in 1995 and won the 1996 American Book Award. Alexie's screenplay for the acclaimed independent film *Smoke Signals* (1998) is based in part on *The Lone Ranger and Tonto Fistfight in Heaven.*

In 2007, The *Absolutely True Diary of a Part-Time Indian*, Alexie's semi-autobiographical novel, won the National Book Award for Young People's Literature. Alexie's other novels for young adults include *Indian Killer*, published in

1996, and *Flight*, published in 2007. In addition, he has written several other short story and poetry collections, including *War Dances*, which won the 2010 PEN/Faulkner Award for Fiction. In 2010, Sherman Alexie won the Native Writers Circle of the Americas Lifetime Achievement Award.

He currently lives in Seattle with his family.

The Absolutely True Diary of a Part-Time Indian Study Guide

The Absolutely True Diary of a Part-Time Indian is loosely based on author Sherman Alexie's life. Alexie tells the story of Junior, a 14-year old boy growing up on the Spokane Indian Reservation. In a diary narration style, the novel explores themes of racism, classism, bullying, alcoholism, and cultural appropriation. It was Alexie's first attempt at writing for a young adult audience, which proved to be very successful - *Absolutely True Diary* was critically renowned and won a number of awards - including the 2007 National Book Award for Young People's Literature.

Sixty-five of "Junior's" comics accompany the narrative in *The Absolutely True Diary*. The cartoons were actually done by artist Ellen Forney and often serve to enhance or deepen the novel's plot. Sometimes, the comics offer supplemental material to Junior's tale, like when Junior draws the different ways he gets to and from school. In other instances, the drawings give a humorous undertone to some of the novel's more serious thematic elements, like a flying white horse meant to symbolize the impossibility of hope for Junior and his Indian peers.

While *The Absolutely True Diary of a Part-Time Indian* is widely considered to be one of the best young adult novels of recent years, Alexie has received frequent criticism from parents and educators for his frank exploration of subjects like masturbation, alcoholism, homosexuality, and racism. Certain opponents of the novel's inclusion in school curriculums also maintain that Alexie expresses inappropriate anti-white sentiments. Many of the novel's proponents, however, recognize the value of *Absolutely True Diary;* Alexie is addressing issues with which real teenagers are constantly grappling.

The Absolutely True Diary of a Part-Time Indian Summary

Junior is a fourteen-year old boy living on the Spokane Indian Reservation in Washington. He was born with hydrocephalus (water in the brain), which has led to a number of health problems. In addition, his large skull, awkward lisp, and thick glasses have made him the victim of bullying from his tribe members - teenagers and adults alike.

Junior's family is poor, Junior explains, and the worst thing about poverty is that he cannot do anything about it. He is devastated when his pet dog, Oscar, becomes ill from heat stroke and his family does not have enough money for a veterinary visit. The only way to put Oscar out of his misery, then, is for Junior's father to shoot the poor creature. Junior runs to his friend Rowdy, who attempts to cheer him up by suggesting they visit a local powwow. There, a group of drunk men beat Junior up. To retaliate, Rowdy cuts the eyebrows and ponytails off Junior's attackers after they pass out.

At school, Junior is one of the few students who is genuinely interested in learning. He is excited to start reading his geometry textbook until he opens the cover and realizes that he is supposed to be studying from the same exact book his mother used when she was in high school. Frustrated with the lack of educational resources available on the reservation, Junior hurls the textbook across the room and accidentally hits his teacher, Mr. P., in the face.

Junior is suspended from school, and Mr. P. comes to visit him at home. Instead of reprimanding Junior, Mr. P. shockingly apologizes instead for how he and other white teachers have systematically tried to force Indian children to assimilate into Western culture and encourage them to forget their own roots. He can see Junior's potential and tells his young student that the only way he will succeed is by getting off the reservation. Junior takes Mr. P.'s advice and decides to transfer to Reardan, a school in a wealthier district about twenty miles away. Junior's parents are supportive of his decision, but Rowdy is furious - he starts to cry and then punches Junior in the face.

Junior feels like a complete outsider at Reardan. He admires a pretty girl named Penelope, but she makes fun of his name. Roger, a star athlete, makes a sickeningly racist joke, for which Junior punches him in the face. Instead of fighting back, Roger walks away bewildered, calling Junior "an animal." Junior goes to his grandmother for advice, and she tells him that Roger will respect Junior now that he has stood up for himself. She turns out to be right.

On Halloween, both Junior and Penelope dress up as homeless people, although Junior jokes that his costume is not too far off from the clothing he usually wears. In order to impress his crush, Junior offers to trick-or-treat for money that they can donate to charities aimed at helping the homeless. Junior ends up raising ten dollars on the reservation, but bullies in costume beat him up and steal the money. He tells Penelope what happened and she is sympathetic, saying she will still make the donation in both their names.

Unable to secure Penelope's affections, Junior soon forms a friendship with Gordy, who is academically inclined. Their connection is based on studying; Gordy teaches Junior how to retain knowledge and perform better on exams. At home, Junior discovers that his sister, Mary, has married a man that she met at the casino and has run off to Montana. Later, Mary sends Junior an email describing how happy she is.

By Thanksgiving, Junior is lonely. Rowdy still refuses to speak to him, so he draws a cartoon of the two of them as superheroes and delivers it to Rowdy's home. Back at school, Junior hears Penelope vomiting in the bathroom and finds out that she is bulimic. Junior offers his support and Penelope opens up to him. The two of them finally become friends, which makes other students at Reardan accept Junior, as well.

Junior and Penelope's relationship becomes stronger and he takes her to the Winter Formal. He is embarrassed about having to wear his father's outdated suit, but his classmates find it cool and retro. At the diner after the dance, Junior reluctantly borrows money from Roger to pay for Penelope's meal. That night, Penelope realizes that Junior does not have any money and that he often walks home from school. She asks Roger to give him a ride, and Roger ends up driving Junior home many nights after that.

Junior decides to try out for the Reardan basketball team, and, against the odds, makes it onto the varsity squad. Reardan's first game of the season happens to be against Wellpinit, the reservation school. At the gym, all the spectators from the reservation turn their backs on Junior, whom they see as a traitor to his tribe. During the game, Rowdy jumps Junior violently and knocks him unconscious. However, Junior's Coach is impressed with his tenacity and they form a bond.

Over the Christmas holidays, Junior's father gets drunk and disappears with all the family's money. When he returns from his drinking binge, he gives Junior his only present: a soggy five dollar bill. A larger tragedy hits Junior's family soon thereafter, when Grandmother Spirit is killed by a drunk driver in a hit-and-run. Over two thousand Indians come to her funeral, as she was a highly respected member of the community. Soon after that, Eugene, Junior's father's best friend, is shot in the face during a drunken brawl. As a result of these tragedies, Junior misses a lot of school, but his fellow students support him when a teacher tries to chastise him for his absences.

In the second matchup between the Reardan and Wellpinit basketball teams, Junior is prepared and determined. He leads his team to victory but afterwards, feels ashamed when he sees his former classmates' faces. He alone knows how troubled their lives are; not a single one of them will go to college. Junior emails Rowdy an apology for his behavior, and Rowdy responds. They begin to banter like they used to. Then, tragedy strikes again: Mary dies in a fire after passing out drunk in her trailer. Junior is devastated.

Despite all of the trials he has faced during his freshman year at Reardan, Junior gets mostly As in his classes. He accompanies his parents to the cemetery so they can "spend time" with Grandmother Spirit, Mary, and Eugene. Junior thinks about all the people he has loved who died alcohol-related deaths, and all the Spokanes who will die in the future.

During summer break, Rowdy comes to visit Junior under the pretense that he is bored. The two play basketball, symbolizing the rekindling of their friendship.

The Absolutely True Diary of a Part-Time Indian Characters

Junior

Arnold Spirit, Jr., or Junior, is a fourteen-year-old boy who lives on the Spokane Indian Reservation in Washington; Alexis loosely based the character on himself. Junior is a budding cartoonist who also enjoys playing basketball. Like the other members of the Coeur d'Alene tribe who live on the reservation, Junior has grown up impoverished and surrounded by alcoholism. Yet Junior strives to pursue his education and transfers to Reardan, an affluent school with a mostly white student body. As a result, he suffers from extreme alienation both at his new school and on the reservation, leading him to question where he truly belongs.

Rowdy

Rowdy is Junior's best friend since childhood; they are exactly the same age. However, unlike Junior, Rowdy is strong, tough, and angry. He frequently resorts to violence to deal with his emotional issues because he is the victim of an abusive and alcoholic father. Nevertheless, Rowdy is a phenomenal basketball player and the star of the Wellpinit team.

Gordy

Gordy becomes Junior's closest friend at Reardan. Like Junior, Gordy is committed to his education. However, Gordy (who is white) has had years of hope, support, and opportunities which have allowed him to excel educationally. He becomes Junior's mentor and teaches him the best ways to study and to retain information.

Penelope

Penelope is Junior's friend and love interest at Reardan. She is white, blonde, and very pretty. She does not pay attention to Junior at first, though Junior eventually wins her affections. Once Penelope starts to spend time with Junior, the rest of their Reardan classmates open up to the idea of befriending him. Penelope's father is a terrible racist and she dreams of leaving her small town and traveling the world.

Arnold Spirit, Sr.

Arnold Spirit, Sr. is Junior's father. He is an alcoholic and often wastes the family's meager income at the bar. He is a decent musician and a very good singer; Junior thinks he could have made a career of it if someone had believed in him. Despite Arnold Sr.'s alcoholism, Junior is close to his father. He appreciates Arnold Sr.'s efforts to keep him at Reardan and attests to the fact that his father has never missed one of his basketball games.

Agnes Spirit

Agnes Spirit (formerly Adams) is Junior's mother. She is an extremely smart and a voracious reader who is capable of remembering every piece of information she consumes. She was once an alcoholic, but she has tried her hardest to get her habit under control. She is fiercely loving and committed to her family.

Mary

Mary is Junior's older sister whom he nicknames "Mary Runs Away". A promising student and aspiring writer, Mary retreated into her parents' basement after graduating from high school. However, once she sees Junior pursuing his dreams by going to Reardan, she marries a professional gambler shortly after meeting him and moves to a reservation in Montana. Mary professes to be happy with her new life, which is sadly cut short after a fire consumes the trailer in which she and her husband are living.

Roger

Roger is an athletic and popular student at Reardan. When he and Junior first meet, he teases Junior relentlessly with racist remarks. Junior punches Roger out of frustration, which Roger does not expect. After that, Roger actually starts to respect Junior. They bond while playing together on the basketball team. After Junior and Penelope start to date, Roger becomes Junior's close friend and confidante. He often drives Junior home from school when he does not have a ride.

Grandmother Spirit

Grandmother Spirit is Junior's maternal grandmother. She is wise, independent, and tolerant, and Junior calls her his "favorite person in the world." She is famous across many reservations because she attends powwows all over the country. Grandmother Spirit refrains from drinking alcohol because of what it has done to so many of her tribespeople. In a tragic but ironic twist, she ides after being hit by a drunk driver. Nevertheless, Grandmother Spirit's last request is for her family to forgive her killer.

Eugene

Eugene is Junior's father's best friend, and he is like an uncle to Junior. He is an alcoholic, too, but he is not a violent drunk. He has a motorcycle on which he gives Junior rides to school. At one point, he was an EMT for the tribal ambulance service. Sadly, Eugene dies when one of his friends shoots him in a drunken brawl.

Mr. P.

Mr. P. is Junior's geometry teacher at Wellpinit High School. Junior accidentally hits him in the face when he throws his geometry book in frustration. Instead of chastizing Junior, though, Mr. P. apologizes. He feels bad that white teachers like him have been systematically trying to crush Indian culture. He assures Junior that he has potential and pushes him to leave the reservation and pursue his dreams.

Coach

Coach is Junior's basketball coach at Reardan. Junior respects his coach and desperately wants to impress him. They eventually build a strong bond, especially after Coach witnesses the violence that Junior's tribespeople inflict on him during the Reardan - Wellpinit basketball game. Coach praises Junior's ability to stand tall in the face of adversity and mentors him during his time at Reardan.

The Absolutely True Diary of a Part-Time Indian Glossary

ambidextrous

(adj.) able to use the right and left hands equally well

aquarium

(noun) a transparent tank of water

articulate

having or showing the ability to speak fluently and coherently

decrepit

(adj.) elderly and infirmed

distraught

(adj.) deeply upset and agitated

eccentricity

(noun) the quality of being eccentric

impending

(verb) to be about to happen, usually something bad

monotonous

(adj.) lacking in variation in tone or pitch

penultimate

(adj.) last but one in a series of things; second to the last

petrify

(verb) to change matter into a stony substance; ossify

Ponderosa

(proper noun) a tall slender pine tree, the most widespread conifer in western North America, often planted for timber or for ornamental uses

powwow

(noun) a North American Indian ceremony involving feasting, singing, and dancing

retroactive

(adjective) taking effect from a date in the past

rez

(noun) slang for a North American Indian reservation

secondhand

(adj.) having had a previous owner; not new

spontaneous

(adj.) performed or occurring as a result of a sudden inner impulse or inclination and without premeditation or external stimulus

susceptible

(adj.) likely or liable to be influenced or harmed by a particular thing

tautology

(noun) a phrase or expression in which the same thing is said twice in different words

translucent

(adj.) allowing light, but not detailed images, to pass through; semitransparent

unpredictable

(adj.) not able to be predicted

The Absolutely True Diary of a Part-Time Indian Themes

Managing misery with humor

As Junior faces bullying and alienation both on the rez and at Reardan, he always has the choice of letting his misery defeat him or trying to overcome it. His survival tactic, however, is to use humor to offset life's most difficult challenges. Junior often describes his tormentors in a sarcastic and flippant tone; when the Wellpinit supporters turn their backs on Junior and the Reardan team, Junior comments, "If these dang Indians had been this organized when I went to school here, maybe I would have had more reasons to stay" (144) and starts laughing. He also draws comics to display his struggles in a humorous manner, poking fun at the fact that he rarely has a way to get to school and can't figure out how to answer the question, "are you poor?" This tone makes *Absolutely True Diary* a story of triumph rather than tragedy, showing that Junior's inner strength helps to lift him up even when he is forced to grapple with one devastating loss after another.

Chasing hopes and aspirations

At the beginning of the novel, Junior describes how living on the reservation makes Indians lose hope. He uses his parents as examples of Indians who did not follow their dreams because nobody ever believed in them enough to support their ambitions. A desire to break out of this cycle of poverty and destitution motivates Junior to transfer to Reardan. Once at his new school, Junior immediately notices that his new classmates have endless hope for the future. Though he wrestles with the feeling that he has betrayed his tribe by attending Reardan, Junior is also realistic about the fact that staying on the reservation would not offer him any opportunities for advancement.

Wealth inequality

When Junior is on the reservation, everyone around him is poor; he is used to it. However, once he starts attending Reardan, he becomes acutely aware that he is from a different social class than his peers. He is used to not having much, studying from 35-year-old textbooks, and wearing worn-out hand-me-downs, but his classmates have grown up with an endless array of resources and opportunities. Junior struggles with revealing his family's poverty to his Reardan friends. Meanwhile, Junior's poverty is just as foreign to his wealthy classmates, who turn out to be much more understanding than Junior had expected. When Penelope finds out that Junior is poor, she actually cries. Roger easily lends him money and gives him rides to and from school. Junior discovers then that the first step towards fostering understanding is being truthful about his circumstances, not hiding in shame.

Racism

Junior experiences racism on the reservation and at Reardan. At Reardan, he is surrounded by white classmates and has to tolerate racist jokes and nicknames, even from his teachers and Penelope's father, who warns Junior against impregnating Penelope and "making some charcoal babies" (108). Then, when Junior is on the reservation, he observes the effect that generations of systematic and historical racism have had on the other members of the Coeur d'Alene tribe. He mentions several times that discrimination has broken down Indians' sense of self-worth to the point where they have begun to believe that they deserve to be treated as second-class citizens.

The Support of Family

Despite the challenges that Junior's parents face (they have both struggled with alcoholism, there is never enough money at home), he continually affirms that they are loving and supportive. Even when the family is going hungry, Junior always has faith that his "parents will come bursting through the door with a bucket of Kentucky Fried Chicken" (8). When Junior decides to go to Reardan, his parents fully encourage his ambitions and do whatever they can to scrape together money to support him. During Reardan's re-match basketball game against Wellpinit, Junior knows that his father will be seated in his usual place and thinks, "Yep, my daddy was an undependable drunk. But he'd never missed any of my organized games, conerts, plays, or picnics. He may not have loved me perfectly, but he loved me as well as he could" (189). On the flip side, Junior learns that many of his wealthy new Reardan friends do not have such involved or caring parents. Therefore, Alexie makes the point that love and unity enables survival even in times of hardship.

Alcoholism on the reservation

Junior is uninhibited when it comes to expressing his feelings about the rampant alcoholism on his reservation. He has seen firsthand how alcohol has ruined the lives of a number of his fellow tribespeople, claiming that about ninety percent of the forty-two funerals he has attended in his young life were for people who died from alcohol-related causes. Over the course of the novel, Grandmother Spirit, Eugene, and Mary all die because of alcohol. After his sister's funeral, Junior cries, thinking, "I was crying for my tribe, too. I was crying because I knew five or ten or fifteen more Spokanes would die during the next year, and that most of them would die because of booze" (216). In fact, it is this pattern of alcoholism that forms part of Junior's motivation to get off the reservation, which he describes as a "death camp" (217).

Living between Two Cultures

Junior's main struggle over the course of *The Absolutely True Diary of a Part-Time Indian* is between his cultural ties to the reservation and his ambitions to educate himself and achieve a better lifestyle than most of the members of his tribe. He faces resistance on all sides: Rowdy and many other people on the reservation call Junior a traitor, even turning their backs on him during a basketball game. Meanwhile, Junior's Reardan classmates either ignore him or torment him for being different. He does not feel as though he fits into either place, hence the title "Part-Time Indian." However, Junior eventually discovers that he does not have to mold himself into a preconceived notion of what an Indian or a white kid is supposed to be like. Many share his struggle, he realizes, and thinks to himself, "I might be a lonely Indian boy, but I [am] not alone in my loneliness" (217).

The Absolutely True Diary of a Part-Time Indian Quotes and Analysis

> *"And what's more, our white dentist believed that Indians only felt half as much pain as white people did, so he only gave us half the Novocain."*

> *- Junior, p. 2*

When describing his painful medical history, Junior explains how the white dentist treats Indian patients on the Spokane Reservation. The dentist believes in the stereotyped and racist notion that Indians have a higher pain threshold, so he only gives Junior half as much Novocain to numb his mouth as he would give a white patient. This type of thinking falls into the category of scientific racism, which is the (faulty) belief that certain internal attributes - like strength, pain tolerance, or intelligence - are inherent in a specific ethnic group. Juniors anecdote about the dentist also alludes to the common racist trope of the Noble Savage in which non-Indians believe that Indians are stoic creatures who do not complain about physical torment.

> *"Seriously, I know my mother and father had their dreams when they were kids. They dreamed about being something other than poor, but they never got the chance to be anything because nobody paid attention to their dreams."*

> *- Junior, p. 11*

Like almost everyone else living on the Spokane Indian Reservation, Junior and his family are poor. However, he knows that his parents had dreams of escaping the reservation and their poverty when they were younger. He knows that nobody sets out to be poor. The problem his parents faced, though, is that they had no assistance or support to pursue a different path than their parents; nobody pushed them out of the only life they had ever known. Junior describes the cycle of self-doubt and the crushing low self-esteem that comes from growing up poor, which means that Junior is already aware of the fact that anyone who wants to pursue a life outside of the reservation will need to be able to rely on a strong support system.

> *"His father is drinking hard and throwing hard punches, so Rowdy and his mother are always walking around with bruised and bloody faces.*
>
> *'It's war paint,' Rowdy always says. 'It just makes me look tougher.'"*

> *- Junior and Rowdy, p. 17*

One notable problem on the Indian reservation is abuse, which is often connected to the more widespread problem of alcoholism. Junior often alludes to these issues in his diary, especially when describing Rowdy's father. Rather than viewing himself as a victim, though, Rowdy shrugs off the tragedy of his situation with specific cultural humor. He references war paint which certain tribes used to intimidate people for battles, claiming that people view him as tough because he takes constant beatings. This shows the cycle of hopelessness that Junior frequently mentions; Rowdy does not even consider trying to change his situation, but rather, he believes that he has no choice but to cope with it. The inherent problem is that Rowdy himself grows up to be a volatile, angry man, thus perpetuating the cycle of violence.

> *"'But I do forgive you," he said. 'No matter how much I don't want to. I have to forgive you. It's the only thing that keeps me from smacking you with an ugly stick. When I first started teaching here, that's what we did to the rowdy ones, you know? We beat them. That's how we were taught to teach you. We were supposed to kill the Indian to save the child.'*
>
> *'You killed Indians?'*
>
> *'No, no, it's just a saying. I didn't literally kill Indians. We were supposed to make you give up being Indian. Your songs and stories and language and dancing. Everything. We weren't trying to kill Indian people. We were trying to kill Indian culture.'"*
>
> *- Mr. P. and Junior, p. 35*

Mr. P. discusses an important aspect of American history, which is that white settlers actively tried to eliminate Indian culture in order to make indigenous people assimilate to a Western lifestyle. There are numerous documented cases of settlers taking Indian children from their reservations and placing them in Catholic schools. Their braids were cut off, and they were forced to learn English and forget their own nation's language. Mr. P. references this tragic history when he tells Junior how as a teacher, he was once instructed to ensure that his Indian students forget their songs, language, and culture. This conversation reveals the early American tactic of using forced assimilation to subdue the Indians and take their land. However, Mr. P. is the one who shares this knowledge with Junior, and it is his guilt that forces him to push Junior to fulfill his potential.

> *"None of those guys punched me or got violent. After all, I was a reservation Indian, and no matter how geeky and weak I appeared to be, I was still a potential killer."*
>
> *- Junior, p. 63*

One of the most arcane stereotypes about Indians is the Noble Savage trope. Early settlers believed that Indians were uncivilized and relied on their basic animal instincts for self-preservation. Junior believes that his white classmates at Reardan view him through this racist lens. Therefore, even though Junior is picked on in

Wellpinit for being a sickly, gangly fourteen-year-old, in Reardan he is simply the product of centuries of savagery.

> *"Man, I've always cried too easily. I cry when I'm happy or sad. I cry when I'm angry. I cry because I'm crying. It's weak. It's the opposite of the warrior."*

> *- Junior, p. 75*

One of the most dangerous aspects of widespread discrimination is that its victims often start to internalize it. For example, Junior feels as though he needs to embody the hyper-masculine stereotype of the stoic Indian warrior, like Rowdy does. However, while Rowdy is large and mean, Junior has always been picked on for being small and awkward. Therefore, he feels as though his frequent crying is proof of his weakness, while in truth Junior is actually more emotionally mature than Rowdy or the other bullies who pick on him.

> *"'Okay Arnold,' Dodge said. 'Where did you learn this fact? On the reservation? Yes, we all know there is so much amazing science on the reservation.'"*

> *- Mr. Dodge, p. 85*

While the reservation does not have the best educational resources, Mr. Dodge uses Junior's ethnicity and home environment against him in order to dismiss the point he is trying to make. This is a common technique that people in positions of power use to subjugate others. Mr. Dodge knows that Junior does not have access to the same level of education as many of his classmates, but instead of trying to help Junior succeed, Mr. Dodge uses this information to belittle Junior. However, it is likely that Mr. Dodge is relying on his position of power to assert himself, because he does not want a student whom he sees as inherently inferior to publicly prove him wrong. Therefore, Mr. Dodge is more interested in preserving his pride and maintaining his pre-established stereotypes about Indians than helping a student improve.

> *"'Anorexics are anorexic all the time,' she says. 'I'm only bulemic when I throw up.'*

> *Wow. SHE SOUNDS JUST LIKE MY DAD!"*

> *(Cartoon shows Junior's father saying, 'I'm only an alcoholic when I get drunk.')*

> *- Penelope, Junior, and Junior's father, p. 107*

When Junior hears Penelope talk about her eating disorder, he realizes that she sounds like Junior's father when he talks about his alcohol addiction. This is an important turning point for Junior, who has been feeling like his upbringing is a barrier between him and his new affluent classmates. However, in this instance, Junior is actually able to give Penelope the emotional support that she needs *because* of his experiences with alcoholism on the reservation, which shows him that perhaps he is not quite so different from the other Reardan kids.

> *"'I'm sick of Indian guys who treat white women like bowling trophies.'"*

> *Rowdy, p. 115*

In his response to Junior's email that he is in love with a white girl, Rowdy argues that Indians, as well as other men of color, see white women as the pinnacle of beauty; white women are prizes to be won simply because of their skin color. Traditionally ethnocentric cultures (like popular American culture) view light skin tone as superior to dark skin tones - and the media often justifies this hierarchy. Over time, some people of color internalize this belief, which is why Rowdy is criticizing Junior's pursuit of Penelope - he thinks Junior sees her as a status symbol.

> *"I knew that two or three of those Indians might now have eaten breakfast that morning.*
>
> *No food in the house.*
>
> *I knew that seven or eight of those Indians lived with drunken mothers and fathers.*
>
> *I knew that one of those Indians had a father who dealt crack and meth.*
>
> *I knew two of those Indians had fathers in prison.*
>
> *I knew that none of them were going to college. Not one of them.*
>
> *And I knew that Rowdy's father was probably going to beat the crap out of him for losing the game."*

> *- Junior, p. 195-196*

Junior is jubilant after leading the Reardan basketball team to victory over Wellpinit. However, he is struck with shame once he realizes that by playing for Reardan, he is no longer the underdog. Junior and his teammates have bright futures ahead of them, yet Junior alone knows what the Wellpinit players' lives are like. He suddenly feels a heavy weight of responsibility; for Reardan, this was only a basketball game - but for the Wellpinit kids, there was much more at stake. They could have used the confidence and pride that comes with a major upset, and Junior feels guilty that his aggressive vendetta against Rowdy has prevented him from seeing that.

The Absolutely True Diary of a Part-Time Indian "The Black-Eye-of-the-Month Club," "Why Chicken Means So Much to Me," and "Revenge Is My Middle Name" Summary and Analysis

Summary of "The Black-Eye-of-the-Month Club":

Arnold Spirit, Jr., or "Junior" as he is known on the Spokane Indian Reservation, is a fourteen-year-old boy member of the Coeur d'Alene tribe with an excess of cerebrospinal fluid in his skull that he refers to as "water on the brain." Due to this problem, he has suffered from a number of health problems, like seizures and poor eyesight. He once had ten extra teeth in his mouth, but they had to be pulled out - and all on the same day because the dentist only does major surgery on the reservation once a year. Nevertheless, the dentist did not feel sorry for Junior that day because according to Junior, the dentist believes that Indians only feel half the amount of pain that white people feel. Now that he is a teenager, Junior's awkward appearance and speech impediment make him an outcast; everyone on the reservation bullies him. He turns to drawing cartoons as a way to cope.

Summary of "Why Chicken Means So Much to Me":

Junior has grown up in poverty; he claims that everyone on the reservation lives in similar conditions. Junior says that most people think hunger is the worst part about being poor. He agrees that being hungry for hours is difficult. However, when on the rare occasion his parents come home with a bucket of fried chicken from Kentucky Fried Chicken, it makes Junior feel like his life is worth living. According to Junior, the worst thing about being poor is his inability to stop bad things from happening. When Junior's dog Oscar becomes extremely ill as a result of heat stroke, Junior knows he cannot do anything to stop Oscar's suffering. He wants to take Oscar to the vet, but his family cannot afford it. Junior's father, Arthur Spirit, Sr., takes Oscar out back and shoots him to put the dog out of his misery.

Junior wants to be upset with his parents for killing his dog, but he knows it is impossible for him to be angry with them. They did not want to kill Oscar, but killing Oscar was cheaper and more humane than the alternative. Junior explains that his father and his mother, Agnes Adams, were both raised on the reservation, and even though they once had aspirations, they have fallen into the same cycle of poverty as many of their peers. Junior claims that this is why his parents are now alcoholics. Junior's mother is a smart woman who once wanted to go to college. She reads a lot and has a tremendous memory. Junior's father is a talented singer who once dreamed of becoming a jazz musician. However, they did not have any support or help to leave the reservation and therefore, they have abandoned these childhood ambitions.

Summary of "Revenge Is My Middle Name":

Oscar's death is difficult on Junior. Junior wants to kill himself after losing his closest companion, but his best friend Rowdy talks him out of taking such drastic action. Junior and Rowdy are very close, even though Junior describes Rowdy to be "as strong and mean as a snake" (15). Rowdy always tries to get in fights. According to Junior, this is Rowdy's way of dealing with the alcoholism and abuse he suffers at home. One night, the two friends go to a powwow on the reservation.

Junior initially does not want to go because he knows that he will be bullied, but Rowdy talks him into going. While the boys are at the powwow, the thirty-year-old Andruss triplets get drunk and beat on Junior. Rowdy retaliates against the three brothers by shaving off their eyebrows and cutting off their hair after they have passed out. Junior likes how Rowdy always sticks up for him.

Analysis:

Junior's life on the reservation has been difficult since his birth. He has suffered from brain damage, has had multiple major surgeries, and suffers from seizures - Junior has plenty of reasons to have a pessimistic outlook on life. Furthermore, he has to deal with rampant racism against Indians. From these facts, Junior's life seems miserable. However, the voice in which he tells his story is sarcastic, humorous, and spirited - Junior's singular perspective is only enhanced by his clever cartoons. Therefore, the tone of the novel forms a stark contrast to the novel's content.

The Absolutely True Diary of a Part-Time Indian is a semi-autobiographical novel. Author Sherman Alexie suffered from many of the same health problems and ill treatment as his fictional counterpart. However, Alexie refused to let his circumstances break his spirit, and, like Junior, viewed his life through a humorous lens. He has stated in interviews that many of the Indians he knows do the same thing because the only way to handle a bleak existence is to have a strong sense of humor. Just as Junior re-interprets the events of his life in lighthearted cartoons, Alexie delivers his troubled history with acerbic wit and humorous energy.

From the beginning of his life, Junior is aware that Indians experience racism in America. When Junior's dentist does not give Junior the correct dosage of anesthesia because he believes Indians only feel half the pain that white people feel, he is acting out of the racist belief in the noble savage trope. This outdated myth holds that Indians are sage-like, stoic figures who are mentally strong and can suffer in silence. This notion taints the dentist's perceptions about the humanity of his Indian patients, thus allowing him to justify his medically unsound practices.

Historically, racist beliefs like the dentist's have led to the alienation and segregation of Indian tribes. The American settlers systematically forced native peoples onto desolate reservations, leaving them to fend for themselves on barren land with little money or resources. This type of hardship has since become commonplace for Indians, and currently, many members of various American-based tribes are unable to escape poverty.In *The Absolutely True Diary,* Alexie often ties the loss of hope and aspirations to poverty, showing how socioeconomic class often remains consistent from one generation to the next. When Junior mentions that his mother never realized her dreams because nobody ever believed in her, he is describing a vicious cycle that keeps many of his fellow tribes people from escaping their circumstances.

What makes these circumstances worse, though, is the presence of alcohol. European settlers and traders introduced alcohol to the native peoples during the initial colonization of the Americas in the 16th and 17th centuries. Some scholars even believe that these settlers knowingly inebriated Indians in order to secure better bargaining positions with them. Many also believe that by providing the Indians with alcohol and supporting the addiction, settlers kept them unaware of their dire circumstances.

Today, the Native American population has some of the highest rates of alcoholism in the United States. This can lead to frequent instances of bullying and domestic abuse on reservations. Rowdy's home life is an exemplar of how alcoholism can affect the tight-knit reservation community. His father is frequently intoxicated and resorts to physical abuse to quell his own pain. Rowdy's father's actions thereby influence Rowdy, causing Rowdy to become extremely violent at a moment's notice. He only sees violence at home, so he enacts this same aggression whenever faced with his own personal problems.

The Absolutely True Diary of a Part-Time Indian "Because Geometry is Not a Country Somewhere Near France," "Hope Against Hope," Go Means Go," and "Rowdy Sings the Blues" Summary and Analysis

Summary of "Because Geometry is Not a Country Somewhere Near France":

Junior describes his sister Mary. He calls her "Mary Runs Away" not because she ran away, but because she has lived in her parents' basement since high school. She likes to ruin things for Junior, including telling her brother how his childhood habit of curling up in corners is symbolic of him trying to return to his mother's womb. Despite Mary's eccentricities, though, Junior looks up to her.

On Junior's first day of high school, he is excited to take a geometry class. The class is taught by Mr. P., an older white man with a large nose and a strange face who has a habit of sleeping through class or showing up wearing his pajamas. Most students like Mr. P., though, because Mr. P. doesn't expect much from them.

After Mr. P. has handed out geometry textbooks to the students, Junior sees that his mother's name is written inside the front cover of his. He becomes agitated with the sudden realization that the school has not updated its textbooks in over thirty years. Junior throws the book in frustration and accidentally hits Mr. P. in the nose.

Summary of "Hope Against Hope":

The school suspends Junior for hitting Mr. P. Later, Mr. P comes to Junior's house, but instead of getting angry, he begins to apologize to Junior. Mr. P. says that he and the other white teachers were once instructed to make their Indian students forget their culture and heritage, and he feels guilty about his past compliance with this rule. That is why he cannot punish Junior; he knows that the conditions he and the other teachers implemented have created a chain reaction that has led to his own nose being injured. Mr. P. tells Junior that he is the smartest kid in his school, which means that he has to leave the reservation. Regardless of how difficult it might be, Mr. P. says, leaving the reservation will be Junior's only chance to realize his hopes and aspirations.

Mr. P. also mentions that he taught Mary when she was in high school. She was a bright student who loved to write. Mr. P. says that Mary dreamed of writing romance novels, which Junior cannot believe. After high school, Mr. P. explains, he saw Mary's enthusiasm and hope fade away. That is why he wants Junior to leave the reservation; he sees the same potential in Junior that he once saw in Mary and wants to help Junior avoid his reclusive sister's fate.

Summary of "Go Means Go":

Junior's parents are surprised when Junior asks to transfer to Reardan, a school off the reservation. According to Junior, attending Reardan High School will give him the best chance at a successful future. Even though Reardan is a twenty-two minute drive from the reservation and its student body is entirely white, it also has a computer lab and an excellent chemistry program. Junior's parents are stunned by his request, but once he prods them, they confess that they, too, believe that white people have a better chance at achieving happiness. Therefore, they agree to work hard in order to allow Junior to transfer to Reardan. Junior is nervous, though, because he knows all the Indians on the reservation will think he is a traitor to the tribe.

Summary of "Rowdy Sings the Blues":

Junior meets Rowdy at the swing set and tells him about his plan to transfer schools. Rowdy does not believe Junior because he does not think Junior has the confidence to transfer to an all-white school on his own. Junior affirms that he is going to Reardan and asks Rowdy to go with him. Junior thinks that Reardan's superior basketball team will entice Rowdy. After all, Rowdy is the reservation's star basketball player. However, Rowdy will not go to Reardan and instead begins to cry. Junior tries to comfort him, but Rowdy hits Junior in the nose and leaves.

Analysis:

From the time reservations were established in the 19th century, the educational conditions were bleak. First of all, the reservation schools were historically run and taught by white Americans, including the teachers at Wellpinit Junior High whom Junior calls "our liberal, white, vegetarian do-gooders and conservative, white missionary saviors" (30). Like Mr. P. says, it was common for teachers on the reservation to have little interest in their students' educational future; they instead were trying to fulfill an ulterior political motive.

Teachers forced their Indian students at these state- and religious-run reservation schools to learn English. Students were not allowed to speak their regional or tribal languages; teachers beat students who reverted to their native tongue. Boys' hair had to be cut short to resemble popular hairstyles amongst white men, and school officials replaced Indian children's given names with typical "white names." This forced assimilation is what Mr. P. refers to as "[killing] the Indian to save the child" (35). He admits that the white American faculty has been trying to to eradicate Indian culture and promote the Western ways of life.

Another reason for the unsatisfactory education on the reservation is the lack of proper funding. Alexie demonstrates this in the novel; on the first day of geometry class, Junior realizes that he will be learning from the same textbook that his mother studied thirty years earlier. It is conditions like these that lead to the grim, hopeless future that Junior so often alludes to while describing the adults around him.

These seemingly insurmountable institutional barriers have caused the Indians on Junior's reservation to lose hope. Many young people, like Mary, have no confidence in their ability to succeed because they do not have a support system or any positive reinforcement. This is why Junior is so shocked when Mr. P. comes to his defense and pushes him to strive for a better life - it is the first time Junior has ever had somebody believe in him.

 Both Junior and his parents express the opinion that hope is a luxury for white people. This is because the white people around them have access to good education and other resources that allow them to look toward the future and see happiness. In Junior's eyes, however, hope is "like some mythical creature" (54). Alexie illustrates this simile with one of Junior's cartoons - it is a drawing of a winged horse flying through smiling clouds with "white" written underneath. This mindset is why Junior becomes so adamant about going to Reardan. He knows he will not be able to leave the reservation if he continues on this hopeless path, so he uproots himself and takes the risk of attending an all-white school over twenty miles away.

The Absolutely True Diary of a Part-Time Indian "How to Fight Monsters," "Grandmother Gives Me Some Advice," "Tears of a Clown," and "Halloween" Summary and Analysis

Summary of "How to Fight Monsters":

Junior's father drops Junior off at Reardan for his first day of school and reminds him that the white students are not better than him. Junior thinks to himself that both father and son know that this is not true and wonders if coming to Reardan was the right choice. As he approaches his new school, Junior is filled with the desire to run away, but he knows that the other Indians will bully him mercilessly if he returns to Wellpinit. They already think he is a traitor, but then they will know he is a coward. Junior reluctantly enters Reardan and meets blonde-haired Penelope who makes fun of his name.

Junior experiences bullying at Reardan, though it is not the same as what he used to endure on the reservation. The Indians on the reservation beat him up physically. At Reardan, though, the white students are verbally abusive. They use racial slurs to belittle Junior. One student, Roger, tells Junior a racist joke to make him uncomfortable. Junior retaliates and punches Roger in the face. Instead of hitting Junior back, Roger stares at Junior in disbelief, calls him an animal, and walks away. Junior is confused; he does not understand why Roger did not fight him.

Summary of "Grandmother Gives Me Some Advice":

After his interaction with Roger, Junior worries that the larger boy will come after him and beat him badly. He wishes he was still friends with Rowdy because a fight between Rowdy and Roger would be epic. He shares his fears with Grandmother Spirit, who says that Roger was only acting like an alpha male trying to pick on the new, weak student. She believes that Roger was only trying to see how far Junior could be pushed. Since Junior retaliated, Roger knows that Junior can stand up for himself.

The next morning, Junior's parents do not have enough money for gas, so Junior asks his father's friend Eugene for a ride to school. The other students are impressed when they see Junior arriving at school on the back of Eugene's motorcycle. Eugene mentions that he is proud of Junior for being brave enough to attend an all-white school. As Junior approaches the school, Roger asks him about Eugene. The former bully seems to have a new-found respect for Junior. Feeling confident for once, Junior tries to talk to Penelope, but she pretends not to know him.

Summary of "Tears of a Clown":

Junior reminisces about Dawn, an Indian girl on his reservation that he fell in love with when he was twelve. One night, he told Rowdy that he loved Dawn. Rowdy pretended not to hear. Junior repeated himself, and Rowdy dismissed his feelings. This made Junior cry, which made Rowdy even more agitated. Junior made Rowdy promise not to tell anyone about him crying over Dawn, and Rowdy had always kept his promise.

Summary of "Halloween":

Junior dresses up as a homeless person for Halloween, which is a joke to him because his clothes always make him look homeless. He notices that Penelope is also dressed up like a homeless person, so he comments on their similar costumes. Penelope tells Junior that she is dressing up to protest the treatment of the homeless.

In order to forge a connection with Penelope, Junior makes up a similar story. He says that he has dressed up as a homeless person to protest the treatment of the homeless Indian population. Once he finds out that she is trick-or-treating for spare change to donate to the cause, he says that he is going to do the same thing and suggests that they combine their efforts.

Junior goes trick-or-treating on the reservation and raises ten dollars. He is proud of himself. However, a group of trick-or-treaters in Frankenstein monster masks beat Junior up, spit on him, and steal the money. The next day, Junior tells Penelope about the attack and shows her his bruises. She feels sorry for him and says she will still put his name on her donation. Junior believes that this interaction will make Penelope treat him differently, but she still ignores him most of the time.

Analysis:

One of the most destructive effects of racism is when the victims of it start to believe what people say about them. This is called internalized racism. Like many other Indians in *The Absolutely True Diary*, Junior exhibits internalized racism numerous times throughout the novel. When arrives at Reardan for his first day, Junior comments that the white students "stare at [him] like [he] was Bigfoot or a UFO" (56). This simile shows that Junior can sense how students perceive him: they think of him as as strange, threatening, and imposing. They do not understand why an Indian is attending their school, and as a result, they alienate him. He soon comes to believe he deserves this.

By the end of "How to Fight Monsters," Junior returns to this motif of alienation by saying, "I was a freaky alien" (66). The first time he calls himself an alien being, he is referring to the way the other students see him. Now, though, he has internalized their judgment and is calling himself an alien. He feels uncomfortable around the white students and comes to believe that he is an outsider rather than realizing that the white students are being closed-minded towards a him just because he is different from them.

In this same vein, Junior puts up with a great deal of abuse at the beginning of his school year. His classmates are constantly taunting him with racial slurs and making comments about his background and his race. This all chips away at Junior's spirit. Junior ignores the bullies because he does not want to pick a fight with them, but Roger's comment pushes him over the edge. As soon as Junior punches Roger, though, Roger calls Junior an animal. This shows that Roger is surprised to learn that his comments do have a tangible effect on Junior; it is likely that Roger has never been on the receiving end of such hurtful words. Roger is shocked that his words agitate Junior to the point of becoming violent. Later, Roger seems to be impressed at Junior's ability to stand up for himself.

Junior has been bullied his whole life. He knows to expect the pain and bruising that comes from being punched and kicked. Yet when the trick-or-treaters spit on him, he feels insignificant. He knows that the bullies want to remind him that he is a traitor, but feeling belittled by his tribesmen is hard for Junior to handle. On the other hand, Junior finds stalwart sources of support in Eugene, his grandmother, and his father, all of whom give him the strength to keep pushing forward. Junior looks up to Eugene even though Eugene is a drunk, and Eugene's comments help Junior know that he has made the right choice in attending Reardan.

The Absolutely True Diary of a Part-Time Indian "Slouching Toward Thanksgiving," "My Sister Sends Me an E-Mail," and "Thanksgiving" Summary and Analysis

Summary of "Slouching Toward Thanksgiving":

Being a part of two worlds, the reservation and Reardan, has made Junior feel like he is not human anymore. Nobody notices him; he does not have any friends in either location. He still feels alienated at school, even though he knows more than most of the students at Reardan. In science class, he nervously corrects his teacher's definition of petrified wood. The teacher does not believe Junior, but a white student named Gordy supports Junior's explanation. Rather than praising Junior for his knowledge, however, the teacher gives preferential treatment to Gordy.

A few days later, Junior arrives home and finds out that Mary has gotten married to an Indian man from Montana and is now living there with him. Junior muses that Mary is living out her romantic novel fantasy by having a whirlwind romance with a man she has just met. Junior is upset at first; nobody ever leaves the reservation. He is ultimately happy that Mary has found happiness, though.

The next day, Junior is inspired by Mary's bravery and asks Gordy to be his friend. The two become study partners. Gordy inspires Junior because of how seriously he takes his education. Gordy teaches Junior how to study better and retain more information. Junior says that Gordy is like an alien from *Star Wars*, but he thinks they make a good team.

Summary of "My Sister Sends Me an E-Mail":

Mary sends Junior an email from her new home in Montana. She writes about riding a horse for the first time and is amazed about how different life is on the large reservation. She writes about her honeymoon and how their hotel suite had multiple rooms. She still has not found a job, but Mary is optimistic. She loves her new life and is happy that she made the change.

Summary of "Thanksgiving":

Junior comments that Indians celebrating Thanksgiving is odd since white people began murdering the Indians a few years after the first Thanksgiving. He does not understand what Indians have to be thankful for. His father, in humor, tells Junior that Indians are thankful that the white settlers did not kill off the entire race.

Junior still misses his friendship with Rowdy, so he draws a cartoon of the two of them in superhero costumes. He goes to Rowdy's house, where Rowdy's drunk father answers the door and makes homophobic comments about the picture. He agrees to give it to Rowdy, though. As Junior turns to leave, he sees Rowdy in his bedroom window. Rowdy makes an obscene gesture when Junior waves to him, but Junior can see that Rowdy has not destroyed the cartoon. He feels hopeful that Rowdy still has too much respect for Junior's drawings to destroy one.

Analysis:

Junior has already encountered racism from the students at Reardan, but in these chapters, adults also target him. Mr. Dodge, his science teacher, does not believe Junior's claim that petrified wood is not actually wood and makes a derogatory comment about Junior growing up on the reservation. This shows that Mr. Dodge is ignoring Junior's intelligence because he perceives Junior to be inferior. While it appears at first that Mr. Dodge discredits Junior to save face, he does not have a problem praising Gordy for giving the same answer. The only difference between these two students is race; Mr. Dodge does not believe that Junior, an Indian, has the right to correct him.

While Junior knows he is smart, he admits that Gordy is smarter. He does not resent this, though. Instead, Junior looked to Gordy for guidance and inspiration. Gordy, who does not have any friends, either, teaches Junior how to study and retain information. Junior relishes Gordy's advice because nobody ever taught him studying techniques at the reservation school. Junior has always done well in school because of his insatiable love for books. Beyond that, though, Gordy shows Junior that true learning requires more than just liking books; analytical thinking takes focus and determination.

Though Junior and Gordy are not as close as Junior and Rowdy, the two bond over their love of knowledge. Their shared enthusiasm for learning makes alienates them from their fellow students - both at Reardan and in Wellpinit. Junior even uses a *Star Wars* allusion to describe Gordy. In previous chapters, Junior thinks of himself as the solitary alien at Reardan, but in Gordy he finds someone who shares the same feelings and quirks. Furthermore, Gordy does not try to hide his differences - he celebrates them. Even though Junior and Gordy are both outsiders, Junior finally feels like an insider when he finds somebody who understands him.

Back on the reservation, Mary's beloved romance novels seem to have become symbols for her life. Earlier in the novel, Mr. P. tells Junior that as a teenager, Mary loved romance novels and wanted to write them one day, but that dream drifted away as she got older. Yet seeing Junior attempting to realize his dream may have inspired Mary to live hers. Like a plot in a romance novel, Mary is whisked away into a whirlwind affair with a gambler. She even rides horses on her honeymoon, mimicking a stereotypical scene from a romance novel.

With the horrendous history that shrouds Thanksgiving, it is no wonder that Junior questions why Indians celebrate the holiday in the first place. In his mind, Thanksgiving is a time when white people celebrate how they used, betrayed, and slaughtered Indians. Yet when his father jokes that Indians are thankful that white people did not kill them all, Alexie reveals the sense of irony that pervades this holiday for many Indians. Junior is the only one in his family who considers the crushing defeatism of celebrating Thanksgiving on the reservation. His father approaches the subject as a joke. In fact, many of Junior's family members and friends deal with the stark reality of their situation by escaping (Mary runs away, Junior's parents drink), resorting to violence (Rowdy hits Junior when he feels betrayed), or by making jokes.

The Absolutely True Diary of a Part-Time Indian "Hunger Pains," "Rowdy Gives Me Advice About Love," "Dance, Dance, Dance," "Don't Trust Your Computer," and "My Sister Writes Me a Letter" Summary and Analysis

Summary of "Hunger Pains":

Junior is walking to class when he hears retching noises coming from the girl's restroom. He asks the mystery girl if he can help, but she refuses. Junior waits until the girl walks out of the bathroom; it happens to be Penelope. She is chewing gum, but Junior can still smell vomit on her breath. Junior accuses her of being anorexic. Penelope proudly admits that she's actually a bulimic. Junior thinks that she sounds like his father when he is trying to downplay his alcoholism. Junior tries to be supportive and tells Penelope not to give up. Penelope breaks down and begins crying. She tells Junior that she feels constantly pressured to be strong because she is pretty and popular, and that she is never allowed to feel vulnerable.

After that conversation, Penelope and Junior develop a close friendship. All of Reardan is confused by Penelope's sudden interest in Junior, but Junior is happy to finally be on Penelope's radar. However, part of Junior feels like Penelope is only feigning interest in him as an act of rebellion against her racist, controlling father. Nevertheless, all the new-found attention has made Junior seem like a viable romantic interest, and other girls begin to develop crushes on him.

Summary of "Rowdy Gives Me Advice About Love":

Even though Junior is enjoying his newly acquired popularity, he is still inexperienced when it comes to love. He sends Rowdy an email and asks what to do about being in love with a white girl. Rowdy immediately responds with harsh words; he does not understand why all Indians chase after white girlfriends as if they are "bowling trophies" (115).

Later, Junior asks Gordy what he should do about being in love with Penelope. Gordy responds a few days later after doing a Google search. He has found an article about a young white girl who went missing in Mexico that past summer. He also says that there were over 200 Mexican girls who went missing from the same location, yet none of them received any media attention. According to the article, the media coverage of the case has been racially biased because it portrays white girls as "damsels in distress"" and "privileged" (116). Gordy then says that Junior's being in love with a white girl is racist because he is wrongfully idolizing her.

Summary of "Dance, Dance, Dance":

Junior often thinks of himself as half Indian and half white. At home, his community sees him as white. However, when he is at school, his peers see him as Indian. His white classmates believe that all Indians are wealthy because they live off government handouts and profits from the casinos. Junior knows the truth, though; his family barely scrapes together enough money to keep Junior in school because the reservation is in debt and nobody receives any money from the government.

As the winter dance approaches, Junior asks Penelope to be his date. He has no way of picking her up, so he arranges to meet her at the gym. He shows up wearing his father's suit. He thinks Penelope will make fun of him, but she thinks the style is cool and retro. Afterwards, Junior is walking Penelope to her father's car when a group of students invites them to go out for pancakes. Junior only has five dollars and knows he cannot pay for Penelope's food, but he does not want anyone to know he is poor. Regardless, he goes with Roger, Penelope, and the rest of their friends to the diner in Spokane.

At the diner, Junior tries to convince Roger that he has forgotten his wallet at home. Roger is kind and lends him forty dollars. Penelope later asks Junior if he's poor, and Junior finally admits to her that he often hitchhikes to and from school. Penelope begins to cry upon hearing about Junior's situation. She runs to Roger and tells him that Junior needs a ride home. Roger generously gives Junior a ride and drives him to and from school many times after that. Junior expresses how good it feels to have friends who care about him.

Summary of "Don't Trust Your Computer":

Junior often misses Rowdy. One day, he emails Rowdy a picture of his smiling face. A few minutes later, Rowdy responds with a photo of his bare butt. Gordy sees the photo and asks about it, and Junior tells Gordy about his deteriorating friendship with Rowdy. He admits that people on the reservation refer to him as an apple because he looks "red" on the outside but is actually "white" on the inside (132).

Summary of "My Sister Writes Me a Letter":

Junior receives a hand-written letter from Mary. She still has not found a job, and she wonders how she is supposed to get experience if nobody will give her a chance.

With all her free time, though, she has started writing her memoirs. She also includes a photo of her new house, which is a trailer. Mary believes that it is beautiful, though, and she is extremely proud of her new life.

Analysis:

Junior is able to support Penelope as she struggles with bulimia because he has been surrounded by addicts his entire life. His father does not believe he is an alcoholic, saying "I'm only an alcoholic when I get drunk" (107). Junior is immediately reminded of his father when Penelope tells him, "I'm only bulimic when I throw up" (107). Junior knows that addicts do not see themselves as addicts, which enables him to sympathize with Penelope's plight. In this case, Junior starts to see his worlds collide; there are striking and unexpected similarities between Reardan and the rez.

When Rowdy refers to white women as "bowling trophies," he is referring to men of color idolizing white skin as the pinnacle of a woman's beauty. Junior unknowingly confirms Rowdy's observation by describing Penelope's whiteness in a number of superficial ways, calling her a "work of art" and "the most perfect kind of vanilla dessert cake" (114). Meanwhile, Rowdy believes that Indian men who desire white girlfriends and reject Indian women are betraying their race.

Gordy actually agrees with Rowdy and believes that Junior is placing Penelope on a pedestal, favoring white, blonde women in the same way that the rest of society and the media do. He thinks Junior is buying into the idea that white girls are inherently more desirable desirable than girls of color. In this way, Junior is still suffering from internalized racism. He sees Penelope's skin as her defining characteristic and the epitome of beauty while simultaneously believing that he is a lesser person because he has darker skin.

Like Rowdy, many of the people on the reservation see Junior as a traitor. They refer to him as an apple, a metaphor which means he tries to be an Indian ("red") on the outside while he is really white on the inside. Statements like these often alienate Junior even further because it shows that nobody in his community sees him as an Indian anymore. He feels too white to be on the reservation and too Indian to fit in at Reardan. Eventually, the lack of support from people his own age pushes Junior to seek new friendships at Reardan.

Junior comes to realize that the aspects of his personality that he feels ashamed about are actually what make him special to his new friends at Reardan. It is because of Junior's experiences with an alcoholic father that he is finally able to forge a connection with Penelope. He is terrified to wear his father's old suit to the dance, but it everyone thinks it is cool and "retro." On the night of the dance, Junior is desperately trying to hide the fact that he comes from a poor family. However, Penelope figures it out and it actually makes them closer. Furthermore, Roger, who was once Junior's tormentor, offers Junior money and a ride. These incidents make Junior feel like he can finally be himself around his white peers, without the fear of inciting judgement or teasing.

The Absolutely True Diary of a Part-Time Indian "Reindeer Games," "And a Partridge in a Pear Tree," "Red Versus White," and "Wake," Summary and Analysis

Summary of "Reindeer Games":

Junior tries out for the Reardan basketball team after his father encourages him to dream big. The tryouts are difficult, as only 24 students will be picked to join. Junior initially does not think he will make it, especially after he sees his burly opponents. Then, Coach pits Junior against Roger in a game of one-on-one. Junior tries his hardest to score against Roger, but Roger is too large and swift. Junior won't give up and begins to play like a football player. He barrels past Roger and successfully makes a shot. Coach admires Junior's tenacity as well as his jump shot, so he gives Junior a spot on the varsity team.

However, Reardan will be playing Wellpinit in the first game of the season. As the Reardan bus approaches the reservation school, the Indians throw rocks at Junior and everyone turns their backs on him as he enters the gym, except for Rowdy, who faces Junior head-on. Junior is nervous because he knows that Rowdy is the reservation's star player and is looking at Junior like he wants to kill him. As the players warm up on the court, someone in the crowd flicks a coin at Junior and hits him in the head. He starts bleeding profusely and has to sit out the first half of the game. Eugene, a former paramedic, gives Junior stitches so he can return to the game for the second half.

During the second half of the game, Junior courageously returns to the court, but Rowdy knocks him unconscious. While Junior is in an ambulance on his way to the hospital, Reardan loses the game and a fight breaks out. Junior wakes up to see Coach sitting by his bedside. Coach praises Junior's determination and sits awake with him all night talking.

Summary of "And a Partridge in a Pear Tree":

Over Christmas break, Junior's father disappears to go get drunk. There is no money and there are no presents. Junior is heartbroken. When his father returns from his drunken spree, however, he surprises Junior with a five dollar bill, which he has kept inside his boot to prevent him from spending it on alcohol. Junior is proud of his father for showing restraint, but he is also upset about his father's absence.

Summary of "Red Versus White":

Junior disputes the claim that he loves white people. He points out problems he has observed in white families, describing how parents (especially fathers) are often absent from their children's lives. Even though he loves his Reardan friends, Junior understands that there are still good things about growing up on the reservation. Junior says that the best thing about the reservation is his grandmother. She is a tolerant individual, he explains, which comes the fact that she has retained her old-school Indian values. Years ago, Indians used to be tolerant of homosexuality and the mentally ill, for example. However, the influence of Christianity and western values has caused Indians to lose this accepting spirit. Junior's grandmother, though, is different. At least she was - Junior reveals that she recently passed away after being hit by a drunk driver. Nevertheless, Grandmother Spirit's last request was for her family to forgive the man who killed her. Her death has been extremely difficult for Junior. He ponders the cruel irony that Grandmother Spirit was one of the few Indians he knew who had never taken a drink and yet she was killed by a drunk driver.

Summary of "Wake":

Grandmother Spirit's funeral is held at the high school football field, which is the only space on the reservation that can hold the 2,000 plus Indians who come to pay their respects to her. Junior is happy that his grandmother is receiving such an inspiring celebration. Meanwhile, the Indians on the reservation have stopped bullying him so that he can grieve in peace.

While many people get up and speak about how amazing Grandmother Spirit was, one person stands out from the rest. Junior refers to him as Billionaire Ted, a white man wearing expensive stereotypical Indian clothes and collectable costume paraphernalia from the film *Dances With Wolves*. Ted gives a speech about how he bought a beautiful beaded powwow dance outfit from a swindler years ago, but felt guilty about purchasing in such a shady manner. Therefore, he spent thousands of dollars to find out who the gown belonged to, and his search led him to a Spokane woman named Grandmother Spirit. After struggling with the decision of whether or not to return the gown, he eventually decided to bring it back to its rightful owner. However, Billionaire Ted is shocked to discover that at the very moment he has decided to return the gown, Grandmother Spirit has passed away. During Billionaire Ted's condescending, pompous, and cliched speech, Junior makes sarcastic comments in his mind.

As a show of good faith, Billionaire Ted asks Junior's mother to accept the gown in her mother's place. However, Junior's mother announces that even though her mother attended hundreds of powwows, she was never a powwow dancer and that the bead pattern on the gown is from a different tribe. Billionaire Ted takes his gown and walks away, embarrassed. Junior is happy when the whole crowd laughs at

Billionaire Ted's expense. For a moment, it lessens the blow of losing his beloved grandmother.

Analysis:

In these chapters, it becomes clear that all of the hardship Junior has suffered has made him a determined young man who fights for every opportunity.
Junior's perseverance is what draws Coach to him in the first place. Despite being smaller and less skilled than Roger, Junior does not give up during their one-on-one match and even manages to score a point with a free throw. Besides his shooting skills, Coach sees Junior's spirit as an excellent addition to the team, admiring his determination to go on even after being knocked unconscious by Rowdy, his former best friend. Junior is becoming more confident in his place at Reardan because of the support system he is acquiring.

When Reardan's basketball team plays Wellpinit in the first game of the season, Junior's two worlds collide in a physical and violent way. Junior has found a place for himself at his new school, yet the people on the reservation single him out as a traitor. In fact, their hatred of Junior unites the reservation - every single person in the gym turns his or her back on their former friend. Junior, however, remains highly spirited and laughs; his entire team laughs with him. In this scene, Junior displays the leadership skills and courage that he has learned from struggling through life. He refuses to succumb to bullying, which is perplexing to people like Rowdy - who seems to follow the crowd.

Junior takes a break from his narrative to address the allegation that he "loves white people." While he has gained a lot from his new peers at Reardan, he also realizes that they have problems. He points out the strength of the community and the family unit on the reservation, finding it absurd that he has never met many of his Reardan friends' parents. Despite the fact that he is frequently bullied and tormented on the reservation, Junior holds certain aspects of his culture dear, most of all his grandmother. Her death is a tragic result of the rampant alcoholism on the reservation, but the subsequent celebration of Grandmother Spirit's life affirms Junior's faith. For one, the Indians stop tormenting him, realizing that he is suffering enough. Secondly, Grandmother Spirit had touched people far and wide, drawing nearly 2,000 individuals to her funeral - including a misinformed billionaire who unwittingly brings some humor into a tragic situation.

While Junior's anecdote about Billionaire Ted functions to unite the mourners in laughter, it also serves to show that many white people idolize and create stereotypes about Indian culture. Billionaire Ted intends thinks he is making a respectful speech, but it is filled with interjections of self-importance that show the Indians attending the funeral attendance that he is not there to celebrate their culture but instead sees this experience as part of his collection of expensive Indian artifacts.

Even then, Billionaire Ted's flashy clothes and inaccurate knowledge about the powwow dress show that he does not actually care about the people whose culture he is commodifying. When describing Ted's outfit, Junior even alludes to the 1989 film

Dances With Wolves, which is infamous within Indian communities for its inaccurate and stereotypical "Noble Savage" portrayal of the Lakota Indians. Billionaire Ted's racism is different than the comments Junior endures when he first attends Reardan, but it is racism all the same; Billionaire Ted may not even realize it, but he believes that he is better than the Indians and by "celebrating" their culture, he is doing them a great service.

The Absolutely True Diary of a Part-Time Indian "Valentine Heart," "In Like a Lion," "Rowdy and I Have a Serious Discussion about Basketball," "Because Russian Guys and Not Always Geniuses," "My Final Freshman Year Report Card," "Remembering," and "Talking About Turtles" Summary and Analysis

Summary of "Valentine Heart":

A few days after Valentine's day, Junior finds out that Eugene has been killed in a bar fight with his friend Bobby. The rumor is that the two fought over a bottle of wine, and Bobby shot Eugene in the face to get the last drop. Bobby doesn't even remember firing the gun but feels extremely guilty once he sobers up. He hangs himself in his prison cell.

Because of all the deaths in his family, Junior misses many days of school. He draws a cartoon depicting all the reasons that he has missed school, including funerals, a lack of gas money, and his mother refusing to let him leave because she is scared to be alone. One day, Mrs. Jeremy, one of Junior's teachers, makes an ignorant and snide comment in class about Junior's woeful attendance record. Junior is too afraid to stand up to Mrs. Jeremy, but Gordy drops his textbook on the floor as a sign of protest. Penelope and the rest of Junior's classmates follow suit. They all walk out on Mrs. Jeremy, and Junior is happy to have people in his life who want to stand up for him.

Summary of "Like a Lion":

Junior is getting better at basketball and becomes quite a star at Reardan. He is the first Indian player to be on Reardan's varsity team, so he attracts attention from the local media. One reporter hassles Junior for an interview before Reardan's rematch against Wellpinit, so Junior comes clean with his feelings: he has something to prove to himself, to his teammates, and to his former classmates from Wellpinit - and he cannot wait to slaughter Rowdy on the court.

Coach starts Junior and assigns him to guard Rowdy. Rowdy immediately tries to dunk, but Junior steals the ball and dribbles it all the way across the court, then makes a three-pointer. This glorious moment has the Reardan supporters in tears and sets the tone for the rest of the game. Reardan wins by forty points, and Junior guards Rowdy so well that he only scores four points. As Junior is celebrating with his team, he looks at the Wellpinit players and suddenly feels ashamed for being so brutal. He realizes that while most of his teammates have cars, homes, and bright futures, some of the Wellpinit players probably didn't eat breakfast that morning, some suffer the pain of living with alcoholic parents, and not one of them will ever go to college. This realization hits Junior hard, and he weeps in the locker room.

Summary of "Rowdy and I Have a Serious Discussion about Basketball":

Junior and Rowdy exchange a few emails. Junior apologizes for beating Rowdy, but Rowdy responds that he will beat Junior the following year. They banter back and forth like they used to, and Junior is pleased that Rowdy is being friendly towards him once again.

Summary of "Because Russian Guys are Not Always Geniuses":

Junior describes how alcoholism has affected his life, even though he has never been drunk before. He has attended 42 funerals, he explains, and most of the deaths are somehow related to alcohol. Despite the suffering his family has already endured, that winter they receive the most painful news of all. Mary has died. While she and her husband were passed out drunk, a fire started and burned their trailer to the ground, trapping the newlyweds inside. Junior's family is grief-stricken. Junior runs away from Mary's funeral and into the woods, where he runs into Rowdy - who is crying.

Summary of "My Freshman Year Report Card":

This is not technically a chapter. It is Junior's drawing of his report card. He has gotten mostly As during his freshman year at Reardan.

Summary of "Remembering":

Junior and his parents visit the cemetery to maintain the graves of those they have lost in the past year: Grandmother Spirit, Eugene, and Mary. The weight of these deaths hangs over Junior heavily, as he knows that many of his fellow tribe members will also die from alcohol-related deaths. He finds solace in the fact that by attending Reardan, he is doing his best to escape that fate. He is proud of Mary for chasing her dream like he did. Still, Junior feels guilty about leaving the reservation and Rowdy behind. He wishes they could become friends again.

Summary of "Talking About Turtles":

Junior reminisces about the time when he and Rowdy visited Turtle Lake. After a day of swimming, they climbed to the top of a high pine tree and admired the view. Junior is amazed that he survived the climb to the top of the tree, just as he is shocked that he has made it through his first year at Reardan.

Rowdy knocks on Junior's door and says that the only reason he has come over is because he is bored. Junior tries to convince Rowdy to transfer to Reardan. Rowdy rejects Junior's suggestions. He knows that he will live and die on the reservation, but he refers to Junior as "nomadic" (229). He makes Junior promise to send him postcards when he travels the world. The two boys then go outside and play one-on-one basketball for hours. They don't keep score.

Analysis:

Junior's abstinence from alcohol as well as his year at Reardan allows him to see the conditions on the reservation more clearly than others. He cites the number of alcohol-related deaths he has seen so far in his life and compares that number to how many funerals his white friends have attended, usually one or two. In this way, Junior's year at Reardan has given him perspective on the breadth of the alcohol problem on the reservation, but it also distances him from his Reardan classmates. They support him and stand up for him, but only Rowdy can truly understand Junior's pain, because he feels it too. This is why Junior never gives up on reestablishing his friendship with Rowdy, even after he feels accepted at Reardan.

However, Junior's aspirations and broadened horizons also come with increased feelings of responsibility. While his Reardan classmates are celebrating their victory over Wellpinit, only Junior knows that several members of the losing team likely did not eat breakfast that day. Others have abusive parents, and one has a father who is a meth dealer. In this moment, Junior's worlds collide and he feels forced to take a side. He feels like a traitor to his reservation by playing for Wellpinit, but he knows that he can never spend his life there, especially after attaining the hopes and dreams he previously thought were only reserved for white kids.

While "My Freshman Year Report Card" is not a true written chapter, its drawn contents give an idea of the type of education Junior receives at Reardan as compared to his school at Wellpinit. On the reservation, Junior was forced to study from a 30-year-old textbook and his teachers sometimes didn't show up for class. At Reardan, however, Junior takes classes in all the basic subjects as well as computer programming and wood shop. This is the sad reality of Junior's position: the Indian schools simply do not have the resources to give their students access to the professional skills that will give them further advantages later in life.

Junior wistfully remembers the time when he and Rowdy scaled a giant tree at Turtle Lake. He shares some local mythology about Turtle Lake, which reveals his pride in his culture and his feelings of solidarity with people on the reservation. He then describes the afternoon when he and Rowdy scaled a giant pine tree overlooking Turtle Lake, remembering, "I was scared, terrified... but it was also fun, you know?" (226). This anecdote symbolizes how much Junior relies on Rowdy's support when he is taking risks. He misses having a companion who understands where he comes from and supports him as he continues on his journey through life.

Finally, Rowdy returns to Junior's front door. He is finally able to overcome the distance that has grown between them. Even though this final scene shows how Junior feels as though he is a part of his tribe once more, it also becomes clear that everyone in Wellpinit, including Rowdy, can see that Junior will not stay there. Rowdy, however, contextualizes Junior's aspirations within the Indian tradition: he is a nomad like their ancestors were before settlers trapped them on reservations and stripped away their hope. By making this comparison, Rowdy shows Junior that he can be an Indian *and* be successful, as long as he remembers where he comes from.

The Absolutely True Diary of a Part-Time Indian Symbols, Allegory and Motifs

Corners (Symbol)

Mary tells Junior that his habit of sleeping while squeezed into corners is symbolic of his desire to return to his mother's womb. Even though huddling in corners makes Junior feel safe, he is squeamish about the image of being inside the womb and changes his sleeping position.

Flying White Horse (Symbol)

Junior draws a flying white horse in his diary to symbolize hope. It is an imaginary creature, meaning that he can only speculate what it feels like to have hope. Additionally, it is white, which underlines Junior's belief that hope is a luxury that only white people have.

Romance Novels (Symbol)

Mary's interest in romance novels are symbolic of her life choices. One she sees Junior going off the reservation to chase his dreams of higher education, she decides to live out her own fantasy of having a whirlwind romance, much like what might happen in a romance novel. She writes enthusiastic letters to Junior idealizing her life in Montana, even calling her run-down trailer home "the most gorgeous place in the world!" (134).

Alien (Symbol)

Junior often refers to himself an alien, which is symbolic of his alienation. After going to Reardan, he is not comfortable being around his former friends on the reservation or his new classmates. Being friends with Rowdy and Gordy helps him overcome these feelings, but he knows that he will always be straddling these two worlds.

Dances With Wolves (Allegory)

In his drawing of Billionaire Ted, Junior notes that some of Billionaire Ted's clothes are collectables from the Kevin Costner film *Dances with Wolves*. When it was released in 1990, *Dances With Wolves* enjoyed wide critical acclaim from American critics and audiences, even winning the Academy Award for Best Picture. However, many Lakota tribespeople have spoken against the film, claiming that it portrays their culture stereotypically and inaccurately to create a more compelling story for Costner's "White Savior" character. The controversy surrounding *Dances with Wolves* serves as an allegory for the way that Billionaire Ted sees Indian culture - he believes that by collecting their art and visiting their reservation, he truly understands their plight.

The Absolutely True Diary of a Part-Time Indian Metaphors and Similes

"as strong and mean as a snake" (Simile)

Junior uses this phrase to describe Rowdy. Rowdy is large and combative. He does not let anyone take advantage of him, and he is prone to using violent force if he feels threatened. Junior's description of Rowdy emphasizes Rowdy's tendency to eschew rational thought and react according to his natural animal instincts.

"like some mythical creature" (simile)

Junior describes hope to be "like some mythical creature." This indicates that he has heard that hope exists, but, like a rare mythical beast, he has never actually experienced it in person.

"like I was Bigfood or a UFO" (simile)

Junior often describes himself as an alien in order to demonstrate that he feels out of place. This simile shows how Junior feels when he first arrives at Reardan; all of the other students are staring at him as though he is some kind of unfamiliar, unbelievable sight.

"They call me an apple"

The other Indians on the reservation call Junior an apple because he looks "red" on the outside but is truly white on the inside. They consider him a traitor for attending a white school away from the reservation. "Red" is a racist and derogatory term for Indians; Junior's tribespeople use this metaphor as an insult.

"Like a Lion" (simile)

This chapter heading shows that Junior starts to feel powerful as his basketball skills improve. In Reardan's second game against Wellpinit, Junior is tenacious and unwavering. He remains focused like a lion stalking its prey. However, after

Wellpinit's crushing defeat, Junior realizes that being a lion also means accepting that he is a predator and he has the power to subjugate his weaker prey.

The Absolutely True Diary of a Part-Time Indian Irony

Roger calling Junior an animal

After Roger insults Junior by saying "the most racist thing [Junior has] ever heard in [his] life" (64), Junior retaliates by punching Roger in the face. Roger is shocked and slinks away, calling Junior "an animal." However, Roger's fear is ironic because Roger is the one who has exhibited a startling lack of empathy in making such racist comments, while Junior is simply trying to stand up for himself.

Junior dressing as a homeless person for Halloween

Junior dresses as a homeless person on Halloween. He jokes ironically, "there's not much difference between my good and bad clothes, so I pretty much look half-homeless anyway" (77). Penelope, who does not come from a poor family, dresses as a homeless person as well. She is doing so in order to raise awareness about the treatment of homeless people in across the country. What she does not realize is that Junior, a person she has made fun of in the past, comes from a very meager background. She is saddened by the reality of vast problem but cannot the problems that are right in front of her face.

Junior wearing his father's suit

Junior is embarassed that he has to wear his father's old polyester suit to the Winter Formal. "I was worried that people would make fun of me..." (122). However, his Reardan classmates are thrilled when they see Junior's outdated clothes. They don't know that he has no other option, and believe that he is making a retro style statement. It is ironic that while Junior is nervous about putting his family's financial situation on display, the fact that he is different actually elevates his social standing at Reardan.

Grandmother Spirit's Death

Grandmother Spirit, Junior's maternal grandmother, is killed by a drunk driver. Junior points out that "plenty of Indians died because they were drunk. And plenty of drunken Indians have killed other drunken Indians." The sad irony is, however, that Grandmother Spirit "had never drunk alcohol in her life. Not one drop." (159).

The Absolutely True Diary of a Part-Time Indian Imagery

Penelope's Skin

Junior has a crush on Penelope, and his physical descriptions of her are often focused on the whiteness of her skin. By emphasizing Penelope's race, Alexie shows that it is a major part of the reason for Junior's attraction to her. "I watched her like she was a work of art," Junior muses as he observes Penelope playing volleyball, "She was wearing a white shirt and white shorts, and I could see the outlines of her white bra and white panties. Her skin was pale white. Milky white. Cloud white. So she was all white on white on white, like the most perfect kind of vanilla dessert cake you've ever seen" (115).

The Indians turn their backs on Junior

Alexie uses aural and visual imagery to underline the unity amongst the Indians when they turn their backs on Junior, a "former" tribe member. When Junior accompanies the Reardan team into the Wellpinit gym, it goes "...silent. Absolutely quiet. My fellow tribal members saw me and they all stopped cheering, talking, moving. I think they all stopped breathing. And then, as one, they all turned their backs on me. It was a fricking awesome display of contempt" (144). This widespread rejection drives home the fact that Junior is the only one of his tribe to have enough innate ambition to try to make a better life for himself, but it also makes the reader understand how difficult it has been for Junior to choose a different path than most of the people in his community.

Junior's Dad's Christmas Gift

When Junior's dad does not have enough money for Christmas gifts, he runs away to get drunk. He returns after New Year's Eve, hung over and apologetic, and tells Junior that there is something for him in his boot. Junior describes the boot as smelling like "booze and fear and failure" and inside, he finds a "wrinkled and damp five-dollar bill" (151). Alexie uses olfactory and visual imagery to evoke the pathetic nature of this scene. The imagery also emphasizes that within this beer and shame-soaked reality, there are many hidden little gifts that help Junior to maintain his faith in the world.

Penelope's Builima

Junior overhears someone vomiting up his or her food in the bathroom. He then describes the "lovely Penelope" coming out of the bathroom "chomping hard on cinnamon gum." Junior can tell that Penelope has "tried to cover the smell of vomit with the biggest piece of cinnamon gum in the world," but she has failed, and Junior thinks she smells "like somebody vomited on a big old cinnamon tree" (106). This is an example of olfactory imagery, and reveals that beneath her pristine white exterior, Penelope is vulnerable. She cannot always cover up her weaknesses, no matter how hard she tries.

The Absolutely True Diary of a Part-Time Indian Indian Exonyms

In *The Absolutely True Diary of a Part-Time Indian*, Sherman Alexie makes a clear point of referring to the people on the Spokane Reservation as "Indians." As the author, it is his personal choice to call his people whatever he wants, and Alexie has always referred to himself thusly. However, there is a long-standing dispute on what to call "Indians." Over the years, official terms have included Indian, Native American, American Indian, Indigenous, and First Peoples, as well as a number of outdated racist epithets that are no longer appropriate. Each of these terms has been deemed correct at some point over past three centuries, but many Indians still feel as though none of these terms correctly identify them.

It is a widely known fact that Christopher Columbus is responsible for the term "Indian" because when he came to the Americans in the 15th century, he believed that he had actually arrived in India. Americans continued to call members of these indigenous tribes "Indians" until the 1960s and 1970s, when the American government switched the official term to "Native American" in an attempt to be more respectful. However, this term has never been fully accepted. For example, Russell Means, a leader of the American Indian Movement, prefers the term "American Indian" because he feels that it speaks more to his cultural origins.

Despite official decrees, much of the older terminology still remains in wide use across the United States. According to an article on PBS.org, "A 1995 Census Bureau survey that asked indigenous Americans their preferences for names (the last such survey done by the bureau) found that 49 percent preferred the term *Indian*, 37 percent *Native American*, and 3.6 percent "some other name." About 5 percent expressed no preference."

Even so, more and more indigenous peoples are beginning to eschew these broad and generalized terms altogether. As different nations work to reclaim their cultures and strengthen their communities, they are frequently choosing to refer to themselves according to their specific tribes. People from the Sioux tribe have a different language and customs from the Cherokee, Navajo, or Lakota tribes, and they do not want to be lumped into one overarching identity based on the archaic perceptions of early European settlers.

The Absolutely True Diary of a Part-Time Indian Literary Elements

Genre

Young Adult

Setting and Context

Early 2000's in Washington State - on and around the Spokane Indian Reservation

Narrator and Point of View

Junior is the narrator. The story is told from his first person point of view as the novel is written in the form of a personal diary.

Tone and Mood

The mood of the novel is light-hearted, as Junior is an awkward but humorously honest fourteen-year-old boy writing in his diary. At its core, this is a coming-of-age novel with a dramatic narrative arc. Because of this, Absolutely True Diary resonates with a universal audience. It is also educational for those who are unfamiliar with Indian culture and the problems currently facing people who live on reservations in the United States.

Protagonist and Antagonist

Junior is the protagonist. Rowdy, Roger, Mr. Dodge, and the Indians on the reservation are all antagonists at some point in the story; the most prominent antagonistic forces are racism and alcohol addiction.

Major Conflict

The major conflict is whether or not Junior and Rowdy will be able to repair their friendship after Junior goes to Reardan. Their relationship is symbolic of Junior's struggle to reconcile his roots and his ambition to build a life outside of the reservation.

Climax

The climax of the novel occurs when Junior leads the Reardan team to victory over his former classmates from Wellpinit; this is a turning point for Junior because he realizes that going to Reardan has given him hope for his future, but his old friends do not have that luxury.

Foreshadowing

1) Junior calls his sister "Mary Runs Away" (27) because she runs away from life and lives in their parents' basement. However, this nickname foreshadows Mary's impulsive decision to marry a man she has just met and run away to Montana with him. 2) Mr. P. tells Junior, "your friend Rowdy, he's given up. That's why he likes to hurt people. He wants them to feel as bad as he does" (42). This accurate analysis of Rowdy's mentality foreshadows the rejection and abuse that Rowdy inflicts on Junior once he chooses to leave Wellpinit for Reardan. 3) After Rowdy shaves off the Andruss brothers' eyebrows as penance for bullying Junior, Junior admits that "revenge... feels pretty good" (22). This foreshadows his decision to play aggressively in Reardan's rematch against Wellpinit so that he can humiliate Rowdy, a moment in which he finally realizes that revenge can be just as hurtful as the action that seemingly justified it.

Understatement

1) "'Uh, er, um,' I said. Yeah, I was so articulate" (84). Alexie uses understatement to convey Junior's self-awareness that he is nervous while defying his science teacher.

Allusions

1) "Tonto" (64) - An allusion to the Native American sidekick to the Lone Ranger, a popular character from the American western genre. Tonto started appearing in serialized radio shows in 1933 and his characterization has contributed to the stereotype of Indians as "Noble Savages." 2) "Prince Charming" (81) - An allusion to the popular fairy tale trope of a dashing, handsome, white royal who always rescues

damsels in distress. Junior imagines Rowdy telling him that he (Junior) is the antithesis of Prince Charming and therefore will never have a chance with Penelope.

Imagery

1) "My hopes and dreams floated up in a mushroom cloud" (31). This description evokes the sense of hopelessness that overwhelms Junior once he discovers that he is expected to study geometry from the same textbook his mother used more than thirty years before. The image of a mushroom cloud is one of complete destruction, as it is commonly associated with massive bombings. 2) "...I could smell his breath. Onions and garlic and hamburger and shame and pain" (42). This imagery invokes Mr. P's sloppiness as well as the weight of his guilt about having purposely squashed Indian culture in his classroom. It is effective in showing how open Mr. P. is being with Junior - he is close enough so Junior can tell what he had for lunch, and he is also revealing the source of his pain. 3) "Those kids weren't just white. They were translucent. I could see the blue veins running through their skin like rivers" (56). This imagery emphasizes how different Junior feels at Reardan because of his brown skin.

Paradox

1) Junior's dad misses Christmas to go on a drunken binge, but he manages to save a five-dollar bill for Junior in his boot. Junior calls the money "a beautiful and ugly thing" (151) because he knows how badly his dad probably wanted to use the five dollars to get more drunk, yet he resents his father for being drunk and missing the holidays in the first place. 2) Junior claims that many of his Reardan classmates' fathers are "good at hiding in plain sight" (153). This paradox invokes the mental absence of these parents, who may be home every night but do not pay any attention to their children.

Parallelism

1) "We were supposed to kill the Indian to save the child" (35). This use of parallelism underlines Mr. P.'s point that many white Americans have treated Indian culture as somehow threatening to American culture, thus encouraging white reservation teachers to force their Indian students to assimilate. 2) "My cartoons weren't just good for giggles; they were also good for poetry" (95). Here, the use of parallelism emphasizes the importance of Junior's (often humorous) cartoons - they are his way of expressing himself. 3) "They were constantly scraping together enough money to pay for gas, to get me lunch money, to buy me a new pair of jeans and a few new shirts" (119). This repetition emphasizes how hard Junior's parents are working to support their ambitious son.

Metonymy and Synecdoche

1) "I kept glancing over at Wellpinit as they ran their layup drills" (190). This is an example of synecdoche because Alexie uses "Wellpinit" to refer to the Wellpinit High School basketball team.

Personification

1) "That old, old, old, decrepit geometry book hit my heart with the force of a nuclear bomb" (31). By personifying the thirty-year-old geometry textbook that Junior is expected to study in his class at Wellpinit, Alexie makes the book a powerful symbol for the lack of educational resources on the reservation. 2) "The grief didn't hit me right away" (201). By personifying Junior's grief after hearing about Mary's death, Alexie gives the loss a physical presence, which reflects the devastating effect that the tragedy has on Junior's life.

The Absolutely True Diary of a Part-Time Indian Links

Sherman Alexie

http://fallsapart.com/

Sherman Alexie's official website

Off the Rez

http://www.nytimes.com/2007/11/11/books/review/Barcott3-t.html

the New York Times' 2007 review of *The Absolutely True Story of a Part-Time Indian*

The Absolutely True Diary of a Part-Time Indian Essay Questions

1. **Why is Junior more likely to leave the reservation than Rowdy?**

   Junior's family is more supportive than Rowdy's. They knew how important Junior's future is to him, and they are willing to do whatever it takes to help him achieve that dream. Rowdy's father, though, beats him regularly. He is not interested in Rowdy's future. Because of the abuse he suffers at home, Rowdy does not have the same hopeful attitude that Junior does; he has only ever been able to channel his energy into violence.

2. **What finally prompts Penelope to become friends with Junior? How can Junior relate to her in a way that nobody else does?**

   Junior overhears Penelope throwing up in the bathroom. When she tries to boast about her eating disorder, Junior sees a parallel to the way his own father jokes about his alcoholism. Unlike many of the other Reardan kids, Junior knows a lot about addiction and self-harm because he has seen it firsthand. This connection is ultimately ironic - Penelope initially rejects Junior because he is from the reservation; yet it is his unique experiences from growing up on the reservation that eventually forge a bond between them.

3. **What is the significance of Mary's nickname? How does the meaning evolve throughout the novel?**

   At first, Junior calls his sister "Mary Runs Away" because she is so "crazy and random" (28). After high school, where she was a promising student with aspirations to become a novelist, Mary "ran away" from life and retreated to her parents' basement. For several years after graduating, Mary spends 23 hours a day in the basement. However, Mary is inspired to change her life once Junior transfers to Reardan. She then runs away from the reservation altogether by marrying a man she barely knows and relocating to Montana. Therefore, "Mary Runs Away" transforms from a girl who is afraid of chasing her dreams to a girl who is willing to leave everything behind in order to pursue her true happiness.

4. **Why is basketball so important to Junior and Rowdy?**

   Basketball plays an important role in both Junior and Rowdy's lives. For Junior, basketball (and his coach) gives him hope and improves his self-esteem after he transfers to Reardan. At first, he feels completely alienated from his new classmates, but he gains their respect with his determination and focus on the basketball court. On the reservation, Rowdy is the basketball star; it the only arena in which he excels. Throughout the novel, Rowdy and Junior communicate through basketball, especially because Rowdy has trouble talking about his feelings. Some of the most significant moments in their friendship occur on the basketball court; Rowdy expresses his frustration about Junior's transfer to Reardan by knocking him out during the game between their schools. At the end of the novel, Alexie uses a (non-competitive) one-on-one basketball game between the two boys to symbolize the renewal of their friendship.

5. **Why does Rowdy criticize Junior for falling in love with Penelope? Do you think he is valid in his criticism? Why or why not?**

Rowdy accuses Junior of being like all the other "Indian guys who treat white women like bowling trophies" (115). Later, Junior's friend Gordy (who is white) comments that by portraying "beautiful white girls" as "damsels in distress," the media reinforces the idea that white women are superior to women of color, which he believes Junior has internalized. Both Gordy and Rowdy criticize Junior for idolizing Penelope because of the color of her skin; they think that his feelings for Penelope are based on the concept of her rather than who she is as a person. Junior's initial descriptions of Penelope in the early days of his crush seem to support his friends' assessment: he watches her as if she is "a work of art," describing her "white shirt and white shorts... [and] her white bra and white panties." He emphasizes that she is "all white on white on white, like the most perfect kind of vanilla dessert cake you've ever seen" (115).

6. **How does Junior's friendship with Gordy differ from his relationship with Rowdy?**

Rowdy's friendship is based on protection and understanding; it is the one constant in Junior's life. Rowdy and Junior know each other better than anyone else knows them. They have grown up together and they come from the same world. Junior knows that Rowdy loves him even when he is bullying him, he understands that Rowdy's abusive home life has left him unable to express himself and that he often resorts to violence in emotional moments. Unlike Junior's friends at Reardan, Rowdy also understands what it's like to grow up on the reservation. He understands Junior's losses and his triumphs because he shares them. Meanwhile, Junior's relationship with Gordy is much more academic and straightforward. They start hanging out by studying together, and Gordy eventually takes Junior under his wing. They bond because they are both outcasts, the only two members of their tribe.

7. **What does Billionaire Ted represent, and why do none of the Indians take him seriously?**

Billionaire Ted is a comedic character, an archetypal white man who appropriates Indian culture. His introduction into the novel gives Junior the chance to comment on what he thinks about "white people [who] show up on Indian reservations every year and start telling Indians how much they love them" (162). He calls this phenomenon "sickening" and "boring." Indeed, Ted treats the mourners at Grandmother Spirit's funeral as if they were collectibles in a museum, reducing their culture to the arrowheads and blankets hanging on the walls of his mansion. However, the interaction between Billionaire Ted and Junior's mother is representative of the fact that even though white settlers shoved Indians onto reservations and stripped away everything they once had, their culture and tribal unity is unshakeable. Just like Junior's race and poor background make him an outsider at Reardan, Ted's elevated social status and racial background mean that he will never truly know "everything" about Indians, no matter how many billions he has in the bank.

8. **According to Junior, what is the "worst part" about being poor?**

Junior believes the worst part about being poor is that poverty kills hope. He claims that hunger is not that bad, because "sooner or later, my parents will come bursting through the door with a bucket of Kentucky Fried Chicken" (8). However, he goes on to describe how it feels to believe that you deserve to be poor. "You start beliving that you're poor because you're stupid and ugly. And then you start believing that you're stupid and ugly because you're Indian" (13). It's an "ugly circle," he observes cynically, a life in which his father has to kill his sick dog because they cannot afford a veterinary visit. Ironically, the lack of hope that Junior cites as the "worst thing about being poor" does not actually cost any money.

9. **Why does Junior cry after leading the Reardan team to victory over Wellpinit?**

The first time that Reardan plays Wellpinit, the Wellpinit supporters turn their backs on Junior and Rowdy clobbers him so hard he ends up in the hospital. This experience fills him with anger and vengeance, so during the rematch, Junior plays as aggressively as he can. When Reardan is celebrating their victory, though, Junior looks at the disappointed Wellpinit players, realizing that a few of them probably haven't eaten breakfast, some of them have alcoholic parents, and that none of them will go to college. He suddenly feels ashamed for being so focused on vengeance; he feels selfish for acting out of pain and anger. This moment is an important turning point for Junior - he starts figuring out how to belong in both places. He is still rooted in his culture even though he goes to Reardan and plans to leave the reservation.

10. **What is Junior's stance on alcohol? What shapes it over the course of the novel?**

Junior mentions alcohol for the first time in the second chapter of the book, when he describes going to a powwow where "the Indians who aren't dancers and singers... are most likely going to get drunk and beat the shit out of any available losers" (17). Both of his parents drink, his father often disappears on drunken binges. All of the deaths that take place over the course of the novel are connected to alcohol; even Grandmother Spirit, who never drank, was hit by a drunk driver. After his sister dies, Junior tries to "hang onto the good and sober moments tightly," but he can't help but cry. "I was crying for my tribe," he explains, "I was crying because I knew five or ten or fifteen more Spokane would die during the next year, and that most of them would die because of booze" (216). At the beginning of the novel, Junior is afraid of drunk bullies beating him up, but by the end of the novel, he has much more perspective; he can see how much his community is hurting.

The Absolutely True Diary of a Part-Time Indian Quizzes

1. **What is Junior's real name?**
   A. Eugene Spirit
   B. Roger Spirit
   C. Rowdy Spirit
   D. Arnold Spirit

2. **Junior refers to his cerebral spinal fluid in his skull as which of the following?**
   A. brain drain
   B. brain grease
   C. monkey grease
   D. brain freeze

3. **How many extra teeth did Junior have when he was a young child?**
   A. ten
   B. eleven
   C. seven
   D. six

4. **At what age did Junior start wearing glasses?**
   A. three
   B. six
   C. five
   D. one

5. **What is Junior's hobby?**
   A. drawing
   B. whittling
   C. science experiments
   D. singing

6. **What is the name of the reservation on which Junior lives?**
   A. Spokane Native American Reservation
   B. Washington Indian Reservation
   C. Spokane Indian Reservation
   D. Washington Native American Reservation

7. **What was Junior's dog's name?**
   A. Oscar
   B. Ted
   C. Rowdy
   D. Penelope

8. **What was Junior's father's dream?**
    A. to become a jazz musician
    B. to become a teacher
    C. to become a stock trader
    D. to become a politician

9. **What was Junior's mother's dream?**
    A. to go to college
    B. to own an animal shelter
    C. to travel the world
    D. to move away from the reservation

10. **To what animal does Junior compare Rowdy?**
    A. a snake
    B. a chicken
    C. a bull
    D. a lion

11. **Who beats up Junior at the powwow?**
    A. Rowdy
    B. Mr. P.
    C. the Andruss brothers
    D. Eugene

12. **What comics does Rowdy like to read?**
    A. Casper the Friendly Ghost
    B. Betty and Veronica
    C. Superman
    D. X-Men

13. **What is Junior's nickname for Mary?**
    A. Mary Little Lamb
    B. Mary Homebody
    C. Mary Runs Away
    D. Mary Quite Contrary

14. **Who did Junior's geometry book once belong to?**
    A. his grandfather
    B. his mother
    C. his father
    D. his grandmother

15. **Whom does Junior hit in the face with his geometry book?**
    A. one of the Andruss brothers
    B. Junior's father
    C. Rowdy
    D. Mr. P.

16. **Whom does Mr. P say is the smartest student he has ever taught?**
    A. Junior's mother
    B. Rowdy
    C. Junior
    D. Mary

17. **What types of stories did Mary write when she was in school?**
    A. children's books
    B. romance stories
    C. mystery novels
    D. literary stories

18. **What is Mr. P.'s advice to Junior?**
    A. leave the reservation
    B. help Mary write a novel
    C. obey his parents
    D. stop being friends with Rowdy

19. **Why does Junior want to attend Reardan?**
    A. Reardan has a better basketball team.
    B. Reardan has a computer and chemistry lab.
    C. Reardan is a private school.
    D. Reardan has white students.

20. **What animal does Junior draw to depict hope?**
    A. a flying white horse
    B. a fiery green dragon
    C. a majestic large griffin
    D. a sleeping pink unicorn

21. **What does Rowdy do when he finds out Junior is transferring to Reardan?**
    A. He hugs Junior
    B. He runs away.
    C. He punches Junior
    D. He gives Junior a $5 bill.

22. **How many miles away from the reservation is Reardan?**
    A. 20
    B. 15
    C. 22
    D. 18

23. **Why does Penelope laugh at Junior on his first day?**
    A. because he has a zit on his face
    B. because he says his name is "Junior"
    C. because his clothes are cheap
    D. because he is not attractive

24. **What does Junior do to Roger when Roger tells a racist joke?**
     A. Junior spits on him.
     B. Junior kicks him.
     C. Junior punches him.
     D. Junior runs away from him.

25. **What does Roger call Junior after their disagreement?**
     A. "animal"
     B. "loser"
     C. "jerk"
     D. "monkey"

Quiz 1 Answer Key

1. **(D)** Arnold Spirit
2. **(B)** brain grease
3. **(A)** ten
4. **(A)** three
5. **(A)** drawing
6. **(C)** Spokane Indian Reservation
7. **(A)** Oscar
8. **(A)** to become a jazz musician
9. **(A)** to go to college
10. **(A)** a snake
11. **(C)** the Andruss brothers
12. **(A)** Casper the Friendly Ghost
13. **(C)** Mary Runs Away
14. **(B)** his mother
15. **(D)** Mr. P.
16. **(D)** Mary
17. **(B)** romance stories
18. **(A)** leave the reservation
19. **(B)** Reardan has a computer and chemistry lab.
20. **(A)** a flying white horse
21. **(C)** He punches Junior
22. **(C)** 22
23. **(B)** because he says his name is "Junior"
24. **(C)** Junior punches him.
25. **(A)** "animal"

The Absolutely True Diary of a Part-Time Indian Quizzes

1. **Who gives Junior advice on how to deal with Roger?**
   A. Rowdy
   B. His father
   C. His mother
   D. His grandmother

2. **What does Junior do that impresses Roger?**
   A. Junior proves a teacher wrong
   B. Junior learns to study from Gordy
   C. Junior collects money for charity on Halloween
   D. Junior gets a ride to school on Eugene's motorcycle

3. **What did Junior do when he told Rowdy about his childhood crush on Dawn?**
   A. laugh
   B. whisper
   C. cry
   D. blush

4. **Penelope dresses as _____ on Halloween.**
   A. a homeless person
   B. a clown
   C. an airplane pilot
   D. a cat

5. **What does Penelope ask for instead of candy on Halloween?**
   A. money for a charity
   B. toothbrushes
   C. fruit
   D. unused clothes

6. **How much money does Junior raise on Halloween?**
   A. $30
   B. $20
   C. $5
   D. $10

7. **What happens to the money that Junior raises on Halloween?**
   A. He donates it.
   B. Bullies steal it.
   C. He loses it.
   D. He spends it.

8. **Why does Mr. Dodge get angry at Junior?**
   A. Junior throws a book at his face.
   B. Junior calls him a jerk.
   C. Junior corrects him in class.
   D. Junior misses class.

9. **Mary's new husband is belongs to the _____ nation.**
   A. Sioux
   B. Cherokee
   C. Creek
   D. Flathead

10. **Where does Mary move after she gets married?**
    A. Montana
    B. North Dakoka
    C. California
    D. Oklahoma

11. **Where does Mary meet her husband?**
    A. high school
    B. a restaurant
    C. elementary school
    D. a casino

12. **What is Junior's role in Mary's wedding?**
    A. Best man
    B. He doesn't have one
    C. He walks her down the aisle
    D. Ring bearer

13. **Mary's marriage inspires Junior to _____.**
    A. ask Gordy to be his friend
    B. become friends with Rowdy again
    C. try out for the basketball team
    D. enroll at Reardan

14. **According to Gordy, how many times does one have to read a book to understand it?**
    A. 6
    B. 4
    C. 5
    D. 3

15. **How many books are in the Reardan library?**
    A. 4,230
    B. 1, 239
    C. 2, 233
    D. 3,412

16. **What food does Mary eat on her honeymoon that she says is as good as their grandmother's?**
        A. corn soup
        B. Indian fry bread
        C. Indian popcorn
        D. pemmican

17. **Junior is confused about Indians celebrating _____.**
        A. Memorial Day
        B. Christmas
        C. Thanksgiving
        D. Fourth of July

18. **Junior delivers a drawing of _____ to Rowdy's house.**
        A. Junior and Rowdy reading comic books
        B. Junior and Rowdy playing basketball
        C. Junior and Rowdy as superheroes
        D. Junior and Rowdy watching television

19. **What class is Junior skipping when he overhears Penelope purging?**
        A. art
        B. computers
        C. math
        D. history

20. **From what eating disorder does Penelope suffer?**
        A. exercise anorexia
        B. bulemia
        C. anorexia
        D. binge eating

21. **When Junior finds out that Penelope is bulimic, he _____.**
        A. supports her
        B. tells on her
        C. belittles her
        D. ignores her

22. **How does Junior describe Penelope's father, Earl?**
        A. He is a quiet man.
        B. He is a good man.
        C. He is a brilliant man.
        D. He is a racist.

23. **What does Penelope want to study in college?**
        A. language
        B. education
        C. architecture
        D. art

24. **What color does Junior associate with Penelope?**
        A. purple
        B. gray
        C. white
        D. blue

25. **Rowdy thinks that Indian men see white girls as _____.**
        A. flowers
        B. gold medals
        C. bowling trophies
        D. birds

Quiz 2 Answer Key

1. **(D)** His grandmother
2. **(D)** Junior gets a ride to school on Eugene's motorcycle
3. **(C)** cry
4. **(A)** a homeless person
5. **(A)** money for a charity
6. **(D)** $10
7. **(B)** Bullies steal it.
8. **(C)** Junior corrects him in class.
9. **(D)** Flathead
10. **(A)** Montana
11. **(D)** a casino
12. **(B)** He doesn't have one
13. **(A)** ask Gordy to be his friend
14. **(D)** 3
15. **(D)** 3,412
16. **(B)** Indian fry bread
17. **(C)** Thanksgiving
18. **(C)** Junior and Rowdy as superheroes
19. **(D)** history
20. **(B)** bulemia
21. **(A)** supports her
22. **(D)** He is a racist.
23. **(C)** architecture
24. **(C)** white
25. **(C)** bowling trophies

The Absolutely True Diary of a Part-Time Indian Quizzes

1. **When Gordy googles "in love with a white girl," he finds an article about _____.**
    A. the death of an African woman in America
    B. the death of a white girl in Africa
    C. the death of a Mexican woman in America
    D. the death of a white girl in Mexico

2. **Why does everyone at Reardan believe Junior is wealthy?**
    A. because of the casino on the reservation
    B. because he wears nice clothes
    C. because he gets such good grades
    D. because he sometimes comes to school on a motorcycle

3. **How much money does Junior have in his pocket when he takes Penelope to the Winter Formal?**
    A. $6
    B. $5
    C. $7
    D. $3

4. **What does Junior wear to the Winter Formal?**
    A. his grandfather's suit
    B. a suit from the thrift store
    C. his father's suit
    D. his regular school clothes

5. **What do the students at Reardan think of the outfit Junior wears to the Winter Formal?**
    A. They think it is a costume.
    B. They think it is silly.
    C. They think it is ill-fitting.
    D. They think it is cool and vintage.

6. **What does Junior's Winter Formal outfit look like?**
    A. It is bright green with stripes.
    B. It is purple velvet.
    C. It is bright pink with polka dots.
    D. It has stripes and polka dots.

7. **Junior and Penelope dance to ___ songs at the Winter Formal.**
    A. 22
    B. 20
    C. 21
    D. 19

8. **What food do Junior and his Reardan friends eat after the Winter Formal?**
    A. waffles
    B. pasta
    C. burgers
    D. pancakes

9. **How much money does Roger give Junior once he realizes Junior cannot pay for dinner?**
    A. $20
    B. $30
    C. $40
    D. $50

10. **What does Penelope do when she finds out Junior is poor?**
    A. She gives him money.
    B. She cries.
    C. She dumps him.
    D. She is angry at him for lying.

11. **Who gives Junior a ride home from the Winter Formal?**
    A. Roger
    B. Penelope
    C. Gordy
    D. Eugene

12. **What does Rowdy send Junior after Junior sends him a picture of his smiling face?**
    A. a picture of his frowning face
    B. a picture of the wall
    C. a picture of a bruise
    D. a picture of his bare butt

13. **What derogatory term do some of the Indians use for Junior?**
    A. an orange
    B. a banana
    C. an apple
    D. a strawberry

14. **In Mary's letter to Junior, she says she is writing _____.**
   A. a mystery novel
   B. Junior's life story
   C. a romance novel
   D. her life story

15. **What kind of house does Mary live in with her new husband?**
   A. a trailer
   B. a shack
   C. a cabin
   D. a hotel

16. **How much older is Junior's mother than Junior's father?**
   A. nine years
   B. eight years
   C. eleven years
   D. ten years

17. **How many students try out for the Reardan basketball team?**
   A. 50
   B. 20
   C. 30
   D. 40

18. **How many basketball teams does Reardan have?**
   A. three
   B. two
   C. one
   D. four

19. **Why does Coach put Junior on the varsity team?**
   A. Because of Junior's free throw
   B. Because Junior is Indian
   C. Because of Junior's determination
   D. Because there weren't enough players

20. **What do some of the Indians throw at the Reardan basketball team's bus when it arrives at Wellpinit?**
   A. snowballs filled with rocks
   B. sticks
   C. beer bottles
   D. basketballs

21. **What does someone in the Wellpinit stadium throw at Junior during the basketball game?**
        A. a nickel
        B. a penny
        C. a dime
        D. a quarter

22. **Why couldn't Eugene play basketball in college?**
        A. He failed high school.
        B. He hurt his leg.
        C. He can't read.
        D. He injured his wrist.

23. **How many stitches does Junior receive after the first basketball game between Reardan and Wellpinit?**
        A. three
        B. two
        C. four
        D. one

24. **What does Rowdy do to Junior during the first basketball game between Reardan and Wellpinit?**
        A. Rowdy trips Junior on the court.
        B. Rowdy knocks Junior unconcsious.
        C. Rowdy punches Junior in the stomach.
        D. Rowdy pushes Junior into the stands.

25. **How many points does Reardan lose in their first basketball game against Wellpinit?**
        A. 60
        B. 30
        C. 40
        D. 50

Quiz 3 Answer Key

1. **(D)** the death of a white girl in Mexico
2. **(A)** because of the casino on the reservation
3. **(B)** $5
4. **(C)** his father's suit
5. **(D)** They think it is cool and vintage.
6. **(D)** It has stripes and polka dots.
7. **(D)** 19
8. **(D)** pancakes
9. **(C)** $40
10. **(B)** She cries.
11. **(A)** Roger
12. **(D)** a picture of his bare butt
13. **(C)** an apple
14. **(D)** her life story
15. **(A)** a trailer
16. **(B)** eight years
17. **(D)** 40
18. **(B)** two
19. **(C)** Because of Junior's determination
20. **(A)** snowballs filled with rocks
21. **(D)** a quarter
22. **(C)** He can't read.
23. **(A)** three
24. **(B)** Rowdy knocks Junior unconcsious.
25. **(B)** 30

The Absolutely True Diary of a Part-Time Indian Quizzes

1. **What does Junior's father give him for Christmas?**
   A. a bowl of oranges
   B. a VHS player
   C. a bag of candy
   D. a five dollar bill

2. **What does Junior's father do over the Christmas holiday?**
   A. looks for work
   B. gets drunk
   C. takes a road trip
   D. goes camping

3. **What does Junior think was his grandmother's best quality?**
   A. her beauty
   B. her dressmaking skills
   C. her tolerance
   D. her quietness

4. **How does Junior's grandmother die?**
   A. She is hit by a drunk driver.
   B. She suffers a stroke.
   C. From her diabetes
   D. She falls down in the shower.

5. **What is Junior's grandmother's last request to her family?**
   A. they should give her a traditional Indian burial
   B. they should give her belongings to charity
   C. they should donate her body to a teaching hospital
   D. they should forgive the man who killed her

6. **What does Junior find ironic about his grandmother's death?**
   A. She had a stroke even though her doctor told her she was low-risk.
   B. She was killed by a drunk driver even though she never drank alcohol.
   C. She was a diabetic who was very strict about her diet.
   D. She fell in the shower even though she usually took baths.

7. **How many people show up to Junior's grandmother's funeral?**
    A. nearly 1,500
    B. nearly 2,500
    C. nearly 1,000
    D. nearly 2,000

8. **What do Eugene and his friend fight over the night Eugene is shot?**
    A. a bottle of wine
    B. a bottle of vodka
    C. a bottle of moonshine
    D. a bottle of whiskey

9. **What did the Reardan students do when Junior's teacher chastises him for missing school?**
    A. They walk out of the class.
    B. They stop participating in class.
    C. They throw wads of paper at the teacher.
    D. They yell at the teacher.

10. **What is Junior's favorite book?**
    A. Jar of Fools
    B. Catcher in the Rye
    C. Feed
    D. The Grapes of Wrath

11. **What is Junior's favorite food?**
    A. grapes
    B. pizza
    C. hamburgers
    D. fried chicken

12. **Who is Junior's favorite musician?**
    A. Guns and Roses
    B. Hank Williams
    C. White Stripes
    D. Patsy Cline

13. **What is Junior's role during Reardan's second basketball game against Wellpinit?**
    A. to guard Rowdy
    B. to make three-pointers
    C. to play point guard
    D. to sit on the bench and cheer

14. **What happens during the first play of Reardan's second basketball game against Wellpinit?**
    A. Rowdy scores the first point.
    B. Junior scores the first point.
    C. Roger scores the first point.
    D. Rowdy knocks Junior unconscious again.

15. **How many points does Reardan score over Wellpinit in their second game?**
    A. 10
    B. 20
    C. 50
    D. 40

16. **Junior is filled with _____ after Reardan beats Wellpinit.**
    A. shame
    B. superiority
    C. anger
    D. indifference

17. **What does Junior realize is the major difference between the Reardan basketball team and the Wellpinit team?**
    A. The Wellpinit kids are younger than the Reardan players.
    B. The Wellpinit kids are not good basketball players.
    C. None of the Wellpinit kids have hope for the future.
    D. The Wellpinit kids are slower runners than the Wellpinit players.

18. **How many funerals has Junior attended?**
    A. 44
    B. 43
    C. 42
    D. 45

19. **How many of the funerals that Junior has attended are due to deaths caused by alcohol?**
    A. 60%
    B. 90%
    C. 80%
    D. 70%

20. **How does Mary die?**
    A. in a fire
    B. in a car wreck
    C. in a hospital
    D. in a work-related accident

21. **What fact does Junior remember about Mary right after he learns of her death?**
        A. that Mary was taller than him
        B. that Mary wanted children
        C. that Mary hated chocolate
        D. that Mary liked cantaloupe

22. **After Mary's death, Junior's mother makes him promise never to _____.**
        A. leave the reservation
        B. smoke
        C. get married
        D. drink alcohol

23. **In what class does Junior make a B-?**
        A. English
        B. history
        C. geology
        D. woodshop

24. **Of which lake is Junior afraid?**
        A. Whale Lake
        B. Dolphin Lake
        C. Turtle Lake
        D. Rabbit Lake

25. **What do Junior and Rowdy do when they become friends again?**
        A. draw cartoons
        B. read comics
        C. play a game of basketball
        D. listen to music

Quiz 4 Answer Key

1. **(D)** a five dollar bill
2. **(B)** gets drunk
3. **(C)** her tolerance
4. **(A)** She is hit by a drunk driver.
5. **(D)** they should forgive the man who killed her
6. **(B)** She was killed by a drunk driver even though she never drank alcohol.
7. **(D)** nearly 2,000
8. **(A)** a bottle of wine
9. **(A)** They walk out of the class.
10. **(D)** The Grapes of Wrath
11. **(B)** pizza
12. **(C)** White Stripes
13. **(A)** to guard Rowdy
14. **(B)** Junior scores the first point.
15. **(D)** 40
16. **(A)** shame
17. **(C)** None of the Wellpinit kids have hope for the future.
18. **(C)** 42
19. **(B)** 90%
20. **(A)** in a fire
21. **(D)** that Mary liked cantaloupe
22. **(D)** drink alcohol
23. **(D)** woodshop
24. **(C)** Turtle Lake
25. **(C)** play a game of basketball

The Absolutely True Diary of a Part-Time Indian Bibliography

Jessica LeAnne Jones, author of ClassicNote. Completed on November 20, 2014, copyright held by GradeSaver.

Updated and revised by A. Boghani April 29, 2015. Copyright held by GradeSaver.

Sherman Alexie. "Why the Best Kids Books are Written in Blood." The Wall Street Journal. July 9, 2011. November 9, 2014. <http://blogs.wsj.com/speakeasy/2011/06/09/why-the-best-kids-books-are-written-in-blood/>.

Alison Flood. "Sherman Alexie young-adult book banned in Idaho schools." The Guardian. April 8, 2014. November 9, 2014. <http://www.theguardian.com/books/2014/apr/08/sherman-alexie-schools-ban-idaho-diary-part-time-indian-anti-christian>.

"Popaganda: Subverting the Holidays." Bitch Media. November 22, 2013. November 9, 2014. <http://fallsapart.com/blog/2013/11/22/podcast-interview-with-bitch-media>.

Britnae Purdy. "Alcoholism, Fetal Alcohol Syndrome, and the Native American Woman." First Peoples Worldwide. August 12, 2014. November 9, 2014. <http://firstpeoples.org/wp/alcoholism-fetal-alcohol-syndrome-and-the-native-american-woman/>.

Andrew Bentley. "Alcohol: It's Different for Native Americans." National Relief Charities Blog. July 30, 2014. November 9, 2014. <http://blog.nrcprograms.org/alcohol-its-different-for-native-americans/>.

"Sherman Alexie." Poetry Foundation. 2010. November 9, 2014. <http://www.poetryfoundation.org/bio/sherman-alexie>.

"Life on the Reservations." US HIstory. November 9, 2014. <http://www.ushistory.org/us/40d.asp>.

Brian W. Dippie. "American Indians: The Image of the Indian." TeacherServe. November 9, 2014. <http://nationalhumanitiescenter.org/tserve/nattrans/ntecoindian/essays/indimage.htm>.

Borgna Brunner. "American Indian versus Native American."
infoplease.com. 2007. November 9, 2014. <http://www.infoplease.com/
spot/aihmterms.html>.

Dennis Gaffney. ""American Indian" or "Native American"? ." April 24,
2006. April 27, 2015. <http://www.pbs.org/wgbh/roadshow/fts/
bismarck_200504A16.html>.

ClassicNotes

GradeSaver™

Getting you the grade since 1999™

Other ClassicNotes from GradeSaver™

12 Angry Men

1984

Absalom, Absalom

A Burnt-Out Case

Accidental Death of
an Anarchist

A Christmas Carol

A Clockwork
Orange

A Clockwork
Orange (Film)

A Confederacy of
Dunces

Adam Bede

A Doll's House

A Farewell to Arms

Agamemnon

A Hero of Our Time

A Hunger Artist

A Journal of the
Plague Year

Alas, Babylon

A Lesson Before
Dying

Alice in Wonderland

Allen Ginsberg's
Poetry

All My Sons

All Quiet on the
Western Front

All the King's Men

All the Pretty Horses

A Long Way Gone

A Lost Lady

American Beauty

A Midsummer
Night's Dream

A Modest Proposal
and Other Satires

Amusing Ourselves
to Death

Andrew Marvell:
Poems

And Then There
Were None

An Enemy of the
People

Angela's Ashes

An Ideal Husband

Animal Farm

An Inspector Calls

Anna Karenina

Anne Bradstreet:
Poems

Anthem

Antigone

Antony and
Cleopatra

A&P and Other
Stories

A Passage to India

Apocalypse Now

A Raisin in the Sun

Are You There God?
It's Me, Margaret.

Aristotle:
Nicomachean
Ethics

For our full list of over 250 Study Guides, Quizzes,
Sample College Application Essays, Literature Essays and E-texts, visit:

www.gradesaver.com

ClassicNotes

GradeSaver™

Getting you the grade since 1999™

Other ClassicNotes from GradeSaver™

Aristotle's Poetics
Aristotle's Politics
Arms and the Man
A Room of One's
    Own
A Room With a
    View
A Rose For Emily
    and Other Short
    Stories
A Separate Peace
As I Lay Dying
A Streetcar Named
    Desire
Astrophil and Stella
A Study in Scarlet
As You Like It
A Tale of Two Cities
A Thousand
    Splendid Suns
Atlas Shrugged
Atonement

A Very Old Man
    With Enormous
    Wings
A Vindication of the
    Rights of Woman
A White Heron and
    Other Stories
A Wrinkle in Time
Babbitt
Balzac and the Little
    Chinese
    Seamstress
Bartleby the
    Scrivener
Bastard Out of
    Carolina
Beloved
Benito Cereno
Beowulf
Bhagavad-Gita
Billy Budd
Black Beauty
Black Boy

Blade Runner
Bleak House
Bless Me, Ultima
Blindness
Blood Meridian: Or
    the Evening
    Redness in the
    West
Blood Wedding
Bluest Eye
Brave New World
Breakfast at
    Tiffany's
Breakfast of
    Champions
Burmese Days
By Night in Chile
Call of the Wild
Candide
Cannery Row
Casablanca
Catch-22
Catching Fire

For our full list of over 250 Study Guides, Quizzes,
Sample College Application Essays, Literature Essays and E-texts, visit:

www.gradesaver.com

ClassicNotes

GradeSaver™

Getting you the grade since 1999™

Other ClassicNotes from GradeSaver™

Cathedral
Cat on a Hot Tin
  Roof
Cat's Cradle
Charlotte's Web
Charlotte Temple
Chinese Cinderella
Christina Rossetti:
  Poems
Christopher
  Marlowe's Poems
Chronicle of a Death
  Foretold
Citizen Kane
Civil Disobedience
Civilization and Its
  Discontents
Civil Peace
Cloud Atlas
Coleridge's Poems
Comedy of Errors
Communist
  Manifesto

Confessions
Confessions of an
  English Opium
  Eater
Connecticut Yankee
  in King Arthur's
  Court
Coriolanus
Crewel
Crime and
  Punishment
Cry, the Beloved
  Country
Cymbeline
Cyrano de Bergerac
Daisy Miller
David Copperfield
Death and the King's
  Horseman
Death and the
  Maiden
Death in Venice
Death of a Salesman

Democracy in
  America
Devil in a Blue
  Dress
Dharma Bums
Disgrace
Divergent
Divine Comedy-I:
  Inferno
Do Androids Dream
  of Electric Sheep?
Doctor Faustus
  (Marlowe)
Don Quixote Book I
Don Quixote Book
  II
Dora: An Analysis
  of a Case of
  Hysteria
Dracula
Dr. Jekyll and Mr.
  Hyde
Dubliners

For our full list of over 250 Study Guides, Quizzes,
Sample College Application Essays, Literature Essays and E-texts, visit:

www.gradesaver.com

ClassicNotes

GradeSaver™

Getting you the grade since 1999™

Other ClassicNotes from GradeSaver™

East of Eden

Edgar Huntly: Memoirs of a Sleep-Walker

Educating Rita

Electra by Sophocles

Emily Dickinson's Collected Poems

Emma

Ender's Game

Endgame

Enduring Love

Enrique's Journey

Equus

Esperanza Rising

Eternal Sunshine of the Spotless Mind

Ethan Frome

Eugene Onegin

Evelina

Everyday Use

Everyman: Morality Play

Everything is Illuminated

Exeter Book

Extremely Loud and Incredibly Close

Ezra Pound: Poems

Fahrenheit 451

Fallen Angels

Fear and Loathing in Las Vegas

Fences

Fifth Business

Fight Club

Fight Club (Film)

Flags of Our Fathers

Flannery O'Connor's Stories

Flight

For Colored Girls Who Have Considered

Suicide When the Rainbow Is Enuf

For Whom the Bell Tolls

Founding Brothers

Frankenstein

Franny and Zooey

Friday Night Lights

Fun Home

Gargantua and Pantagruel

Goethe's Faust

Gorilla, My Love

Great Expectations

Grendel

Gulliver's Travels

Hamlet

Hard Times

Haroun and the Sea of Stories

Harry Potter and the Philosopher's Stone

For our full list of over 250 Study Guides, Quizzes,
Sample College Application Essays, Literature Essays and E-texts, visit:

www.gradesaver.com

ClassicNotes

GradeSaver™

Getting you the grade since 1999™

Other ClassicNotes from GradeSaver™

Heart of Darkness
Hedda Gabler
Henry IV Part 1
Henry IV Part 2
Henry IV
  (Pirandello)
Henry V
Herzog
Hippolytus
Homo Faber
House of Mirth
House on Mango
  Street
Howards End
How the Garcia
  Girls Lost Their
  Accents
I, Claudius
I Know Why the
  Caged Bird Sings
Iliad
Incidents in the Life
  of a Slave Girl

In Cold Blood
Inherit the Wind
In Our Time
Insurgent
Interpreter of
  Maladies
In the Skin of a Lion
In the Time of the
  Butterflies
Into the Wild
Invisible Man
Ishmael
Island of the Blue
  Dolphins
I Will Marry When I
  Want
James and the Giant
  Peach
Jane Eyre
Jazz
John Donne: Poems
Johnny Tremain

Jorge Borges: Short
  Stories
Joseph Andrews
Jude the Obscure
Julius Caesar
Jungle of Cities
Juno and the
  Paycock
Kama Sutra
Kate Chopin's Short
  Stories
Keats' Poems and
  Letters
Kidnapped
King Lear
King Solomon's
  Mines
Kokoro
Kurt Vonnegut's
  Short Stories
Lancelot: Or, the
  Knight of the Cart

For our full list of over 250 Study Guides, Quizzes,
Sample College Application Essays, Literature Essays and E-texts, visit:

www.gradesaver.com

ClassicNotes

GrΛdeSaver™

Getting you the grade since 1999™

Other ClassicNotes from GradeSaver™

Langston Hughes:
    Poems
Last of the
    Mohicans
Leaves of Grass
Left to Tell
Legend
Le Morte d'Arthur
Letter From
    Birmingham Jail
Leviathan
Libation Bearers
Life is Beautiful
Life of Pi
Light In August
Like Water for
    Chocolate
Little Women
Lolita
Long Day's Journey
    Into Night
Look Back in Anger
Looking for Alaska

Lord Byron's Poems
Lord Jim
Lord of the Flies
Love in the Time of
    Cholera
Love Medicine
Lucy
Macbeth
Madame Bovary
Maestro
Maggie: A Girl of
    the Streets and
    Other Stories
Manhattan Transfer
Mankind: Medieval
    Morality Plays
Mansfield Park
Mary Barton
Master Harold...
    And the Boys
Matthew Arnold:
    Poems
MAUS

Measure for
    Measure
Medea
Merchant of Venice
Metamorphoses
Midaq Alley
Middlemarch
Middlesex
Midnight's Children
Moby Dick
Mockingjay
Moll Flanders
Mother Courage and
    Her Children
Mrs. Dalloway
Mrs. Warren's
    Profession
Much Ado About
    Nothing
Murder in the
    Cathedral
My Antonia
Mythology

For our full list of over 250 Study Guides, Quizzes,
Sample College Application Essays, Literature Essays and E-texts, visit:

www.gradesaver.com

ClassicNotes

GrAdeSaver™

Getting you the grade since 1999™

Other ClassicNotes from GradeSaver™

Pudd'nhead Wilson
Purple Hibiscus
Pygmalion
Rabbit, Run
Ray Bradbury: Short
   Stories
Rebecca
Regeneration
Return of the Native
Rhinoceros
Richard II
Richard III
Rip Van Winkle and
   Other Stories
Robert Browning:
   Poems
Robert Frost: Poems
Robinson Crusoe
Roll of Thunder,
   Hear My Cry
Roman Fever and
   Other Stories
Romeo and Juliet

Roots
Rosencrantz and
   Guildenstern Are
   Dead
Rudyard Kipling:
   Poems
Salome
Schindler's List
Season of Migration
   to the North
Second Treatise of
   Government
Secret Sharer
Self Reliance and
   Other Essays
Sense and
   Sensibility
Shakespeare's
   Sonnets
Shantaram
She Stoops to
   Conquer

Short Stories of
   Ernest
   Hemingway
Short Stories of F.
   Scott Fitzgerald
Siddhartha
Silas Marner
Silence
Sir Gawain and the
   Green Knight
Sir Thomas Wyatt:
   Poems
Sister Carrie
Six Characters in
   Search of an
   Author
Slaughterhouse Five
Snow Falling on
   Cedars
Something Wicked
   This Way Comes
Song of Roland
Song of Solomon

For our full list of over 250 Study Guides, Quizzes,
Sample College Application Essays, Literature Essays and E-texts, visit:

www.gradesaver.com

ClassicNotes

Getting you the grade since 1999™

Other ClassicNotes from GradeSaver™

Songs of Innocence and of Experience
Sonny's Blues
Sons and Lovers
Speak
Spenser's Amoretti and Epithalamion
Spring Awakening
Sula
Sundiata: An Epic of Old Mali
Sylvia Plath: Poems
Symposium by Plato
Tartuffe
Tell Me a Riddle
Tender is the Night
Tennyson's Poems
Tess of the D'Urbervilles
The Absolutely True Diary of a Part-Time Indian

The Adventures of Augie March
The Adventures of Huckleberry Finn
The Adventures of Tom Sawyer
The Aeneid
The Age of Innocence
The Alchemist (Coelho)
The Alchemist (Jonson)
The Ambassadors
The Analects of Confucius
The Arabian Nights: One Thousand and One Nights
The Autobiography of an Ex-Colored Man
The Awakening

The Bacchae
The Bean Trees
The Beggar's Opera
The Bell Jar
The Birthday Party
The Bloody Chamber
The Bonfire of the Vanities
The Book of Daniel
The Book of the Duchess and Other Poems
The Book Thief
The Boy in the Striped Pajamas
The Brief Wondrous Life of Oscar Wao
The Brothers Karamazov
The Burning Plain and Other Stories

For our full list of over 250 Study Guides, Quizzes,
Sample College Application Essays, Literature Essays and E-texts, visit:

www.gradesaver.com

ClassicNotes

GrAdeSaver™

Getting you the grade since 1999™

Other ClassicNotes from GradeSaver™

The Canterbury Tales

The Caretaker

The Catcher in the Rye

The Caucasian Chalk Circle

The Cherry Orchard

The Chocolate War

The Chosen

The Chrysanthemums

The Circle

The Collector

The Color of Water

The Color Purple

The Consolation of Philosophy

The Coquette

The Count of Monte Cristo

The Country of the Pointed Firs and Other Stories

The Country Wife

The Crucible

The Crying of Lot 49

The Curious Incident of the Dog in the Night-time

The Death of Ivan Ilych

The Devil and Tom Walker

The Devil's Arithmetic

The Diary of a Young Girl by Anne Frank

The Duchess of Malfi

The Electric Kool-Aid Acid Test

The English Patient

The Epic of Gilgamesh

The Eumenides

The Faerie Queene

The Fall of the House of Usher

The Federalist Papers

The Five People You Meet in Heaven

The Fountainhead

The Frogs

The Garden Party

The Giver

The Glass Castle

The Glass Menagerie

The Godfather

The God of Small Things

For our full list of over 250 Study Guides, Quizzes,
Sample College Application Essays, Literature Essays and E-texts, visit:

www.gradesaver.com

ClassicNotes

GradeSaver™

Getting you the grade since 1999™

Other ClassicNotes from GradeSaver™

The Good Earth

The Good Woman of Setzuan

The Grapes of Wrath

The Great Gatsby

The Guest

The Handmaid's Tale

The Heart of the Matter

The Hiding Place

The History Boys

The History of Rasselas: Prince of Abissinia

The History of Tom Jones, a Foundling

The Hobbit

The Hot Zone

The Hound of the Baskervilles

The House of Bernarda Alba

The House of the Seven Gables

The House of the Spirits

The Hunger Games

The Importance of Being Earnest

Their Eyes Were Watching God

The Island of Dr. Moreau

The Jew of Malta

The Joy Luck Club

The Jungle

The Kite Runner

The Lais of Marie de France

The Legend of Sleepy Hollow

The Life of Olaudah Equiano

The Lion, the Witch and the Wardrobe

The Lone Ranger and Tonto Fistfight in Heaven

The Lord of the Rings: The Fellowship of the Ring

The Lord of the Rings: The Return of the King

The Lord of the Rings: The Two Towers

The Lottery and Other Stories

The Lovely Bones

The Love Song of J. Alfred Prufrock

The Marrow of Tradition

For our full list of over 250 Study Guides, Quizzes,
Sample College Application Essays, Literature Essays and E-texts, visit:

www.gradesaver.com

ClassicNotes

Getting you the grade since 1999™

Other ClassicNotes from GradeSaver™

The Sorrows of
Young Werther
The Souls of Black
Folk
The Sound and the
Fury
The Sound of Waves
The Sovereignty and
Goodness of God
The Spanish
Tragedy
The Spirit Catches
You and You Fall
Down
The Stranger
The Sun Also Rises
The Taming of the
Shrew
The Tempest
The Testing
The Theory of
Moral Sentiments

The Things They
Carried
The Threepenny
Opera
The Time Machine
The Tortilla Curtain
The Trials of
Brother Jero
The Truman Show
The Turn of the
Screw
The Vicar of
Wakefield
The Visit
The Wars
The Waste Land
The Watsons Go to
Birmingham -
1963
The Wave
The Wealth of
Nations
The Whale Rider

The White Devil
The White Tiger
The Wind in the
Willows
The Winter's Tale
The Woman Warrior
The Wonderful
Wizard of Oz
The Yellow
Wallpaper
The Zoo Story
Things Fall Apart
Three Cups of Tea
Three Men in a Boat
(To Say Nothing
of the Dog)
Through the
Looking Glass
Thus Spoke
Zarathustra
Titus Andronicus
To Build a Fire

For our full list of over 250 Study Guides, Quizzes,
Sample College Application Essays, Literature Essays and E-texts, visit:

www.gradesaver.com

Made in the USA
Middletown, DE
25 September 2018